WHAT PEOPLE

INTENTIO

T0058431

For the patient with chronic disease, whether it is manifested as chronic fatigue, fibromyalgia, and/or chemical sensitivity, achieving wellness can be a lifetime's struggle. Patients may look for years before they find the key to their health and well-being. This book is an inspiring story of one woman's desire and ability, not only to achieve good health, but also to discover and develop her God given but latent talents in order to take her place in life as a spiritual healer.
William J. Rea, M.D., F.A.C.S., F.A.A.E.M.
Founder and Director of the Environmental Health Center-Dallas

Can you imagine healing? Can you imagine what it would feel like to be deeply connected to the higher order of your inner self, and to know the entire Universe is organized around your well-being? Can you stretch your boundaries and allow the awakening of dormant parts of you just waiting to come alive? How deeply satisfying that can be! This is what you will find in Jennie Sherwin's book, *Intentional Healing: One Woman's Path to Higher Consciousness and Freedom from Environmental and Other Chronic Illnesses*. It is a beautifully written personal story of the deep healing of her life.
Deborah Singleton, Founder and President of Arasini Foundation; Founder and Director of A Healing Place

Having recovered from the same illness as Jennie, I admire her ability to tell the story of one of the most unbelievable illnesses. Although our healing journeys took us along different paths, one of its great benefits was that it taught us every symptom has a cause and the cure. And it's not a deficiency of the latest drug and device. As a medical doctor for over 40 years, the illness was a gift that fueled me to show others how to heal, regardless of disease label and complete with scientific backup. Thanks to Jennie, many who think that they are undiagnosable or unable to heal will learn it's just not true.

Sherry A. Rogers, M.D., ABFP, ABEM, FACAAI, FACN, author of *Is Your Cardiologist Killing You?*, *Detoxify Or Die*, *The High Blood Pressure Hoax*, *Pain Free In 6 Weeks*, and 12 others (prestigepub lishing.com)

In *Intentional Healing*, Jennie Sherwin has written an inspiring book about her struggle with environment illness, one of the most troubling and disabling illnesses of the twentieth century.

Leo Galland, M.D.

Intentional Healing

One Woman's Path to Higher
Consciousness and Freedom
from Environmental and Other
Chronic Illnesses

Intentional Healing

One Woman's Path to Higher
Consciousness and Freedom
from Environmental and Other
Chronic Illnesses

Jennie Sherwin

CHANGEMAKERS
BOOKS

Winchester, UK
Washington, USA

First published by Changemakers Books, 2012
Changemakers Books is an imprint of John Hunt Publishing Ltd., Laurel House, Station Approach,
Alresford, Hants, SO24 9JH, UK
office1@jhpbooks.net
www.johnhuntpublishing.com
www.changemakers-books.com

For distributor details and how to order please visit the 'Ordering' section on our website.

Text copyright: Jennie Sherwin 2011

ISBN: 978 1 84694 871 8

A CIP catalogue record for this book is available from the British Library.

Design: Stuart Davies

Printed in the USA by Edwards Brothers Malloy

We operate a distinctive and ethical publishing philosophy in all
areas of our business, from our global network of authors to
production and worldwide distribution.

CONTENTS

To Roger

AUTHOR STATEMENT

All healing paths, while they share certain things in common, are unique to the individual. What worked for me might not work for another person. I am not a physician, and nothing I have written should be construed in any way as medical advice. All decisions about physical and mental health should be made in consultation with one's physician or other licensed or certified health care practitioner. In telling my story I am simply sharing my experiences and observations.

FOREWORD

For the patient with chronic disease, whether it is manifested as chronic fatigue, fibromyalgia, and/or chemical sensitivity, achieving wellness can be a lifetime's struggle. Patients may look for years before they find the key to their health and well-being. This book is an inspiring story of one woman's desire and ability, not only to achieve good health, but also to discover and develop her God given but latent talents in order to take her place in life as a spiritual healer.

Jennie's healing journey concisely demonstrates the practical approaches to environmental illness of environmental medicine and energy manipulation that have been shown to be successful in addressing the body's negative responses to chemical injury. These responses are highly individual, being mediated by a person's biochemical makeup, as well as by the combined phenomena of *hormesis* (stimulation or suppression by an extremely low concentration of a toxic substance), *bipolar response* to the same stimulus as its effects spread throughout the body, *distal response* to nerve injury (hypersensitivity in a nerve beyond the injury), and the *masking* of triggering agents and sensitivities through the overloading of the body's ability to detoxify itself of common pollutants.

To overcome these phenomena, Jennie embarked on a supervised detoxification program of progressively longer saunas, taking injections to neutralize her body's reactions to the substances to which she was sensitive, drinking less polluted spring water, eating a rotary diet of organic foods, receiving supplements of vitamins and minerals, and avoiding triggering agents. She moved to an environmentally safer house in the mountains where she could breathe and exercise in clean air. She dealt with the trauma she suffered through a lifetime of chronic illness, as well as the emotional stressors she encountered in the events of her life, through psychotherapeutic consultations with Dr. Carol Cole. When her perception of electromagnetic waves changed, she sought and received energy balancing treatments from Deborah Singleton and her healing team. With their help, she began to view her heightened sensitivities as higher perceptive abilities to guide both herself and others more successfully through life.

Jennie's journey to health through the travails of conquering chemical sensitivity has led her to become the complete being we all would like to be on this earth. She accomplished this by adopting the practices and principles of both environmental medicine and energy balancing, as taught to her by Deborah and her healing team. When society learns how to use the healing practices and principles Jennie followed, people, for the most part, will be able to live a fully engaged life, free of medications, answering many of life's challenges with a vigorous positive response and a healthy outlook for their time on the earth.

William J. Rea, M.D., F.A.C.S., F.A.A.E.M.
Founder and Director of the Environmental Health Center-Dallas

PREFACE

Can you imagine healing? Can you imagine what it would feel like to be deeply connected to the higher order of your inner self, and to know the entire Universe is organized around your well-being? Can you stretch your boundaries and allow the awakening of dormant parts of you just waiting to come alive? How deeply satisfying that can be! This is what you will find in Jennie Sherwin's book, *Intentional Healing: One Woman's Path to Higher Consciousness and Freedom from Environmental and Other Chronic Illnesses*. It is a beautifully written personal story of the deep healing of her life.

Illness can be an invitation to redirect one's life. It can be a time to seek a different interpretation of life, to accept the inner quiet, choose compassion for self, and learn what it means to create wholeness.

The task and the path of healing are both burden and blessing. They require looking deeply within and letting go of the past, which can be filled with judgments, resentments, guilt, and other fears that have kept us in unhealthy thought and emotional patterns, contributing to our illness. Beneath it all are the fruits of new growth, just waiting to be harvested: hope, joy, and the feeling of life-giving energy for oneself and the desire to share it with others.

This is all too difficult to believe when you are suffering, especially with strange and unusual symptoms, and every doctor you consult is unable to pinpoint the source of your symptoms. Jennie Sherwin's book is such a story, wonderfully told, that takes you step by step into how her body and spirit came together, not only to heal her of environmental illness, but also to propel her into a new healthy life full of potential and the desire to serve others.

Because I am a grandmother I have the privilege to relive

3

fairy tales with my granddaughters. Jennie's story reminds me of the tale told in *The Princess and the Goblin*, written by George MacDonald. As the story goes, the young princess, Irene, is exploring the castle when she encounters a woman spinning thread, who introduces herself as the princess's great grandmother. After a time the grandmother gives her a ring and tells her it is attached to an invisible thread. The grandmother tells her that this thread will guide her through the challenges she may meet in life. As you travel with Jennie through her story you will see that its unfolding leads her through one challenge after another, always to come to a wonderful view of wholeness within her and appreciation of her soul's journey. Jennie's trust of the Source is her "invisible thread," to which she comes back again and again.

In reading Jennie's story you will see that she uses traditional Western medicine in combination with many other healing concepts for her personal healing. She shares in clear, simple language the many methods she has used and is still using. Her book will be a wonderful source for those seeking to combine Western medical treatment with other healing approaches.

It has been a privilege and an honor to travel with Jennie on her healing journey. It is a true, exciting story and a great blessing that she has shared with us. Jennie is a gifted writer, a teacher who has lived the journey, and I think we will be hearing more from her.

Deborah Singleton
Founder and President of Arasini Foundation; Founder and Director of A Healing Place

ACKNOWLEDGMENTS

My healing, and this book, would not have been possible without the help of my family, my friends, and the people I met on my healing journey. To my husband, Roger, however, goes the lion's share of my gratitude. He did what I think many Western-trained physicians could never have done. Despite his many years as a leader in evidence-based medicine, he not only let me walk my path to healing in my own way but also supported me through a transformational process that was outside his range of experience. I'm not sure I could have done the same for him, had our roles been reversed. My son, Colin, helped me retain a balanced perspective of who I was as I struggled through the depersonalizing changes I had to institute in my life, while practicing avoidance after the onset of symptoms of chemical sensitivity. My parents, now deceased, who were struggling with illness and aging, bought and shipped clothing to me when I had to avoid clothing stores. My sister, Arleen, provided both emotional and practical support before, during, and after my seven-month treatment in Dallas, despite her grueling schedule as a Ph.D. student. My brother, Bill, his wife, Cheryl, and their children willingly de-scented themselves in order to visit me when I lived in environmental isolation in Dallas during treatment. My aunt, Dorothy, and her husband, Bill, provided their love and support through the five-minute telephone conversations I could manage at the height of my EMF sensitivity. My friends Anita and Susan corresponded with me through cards and letters during the time I could not use a computer or a telephone. Wendy Marquer, Roger's secretary at Tulane, provided invaluable support while I was in treatment. Kelly de Barros, Roger's colleague and longtime friend (who became my friend as well) not only supported Roger at Tulane, but also de-scented herself and visited me in Santa Fe to provide company while Roger was finishing his last semester at Tulane. The other patients I met while in treatment and their partners: Anne Reach and Paul Mogensen, Kathy and Rick Treat, Phyllis and Joe Bauman, Libby Rafert, Susi Lippuner, Beverly and Dick Pape, Loretta Carr, Dian and Frasier Snowden, to name just a few, provided the kind of support that only someone with firsthand knowledge of environmental illness could. Earl Remmel and his wife, Vickie, owners and managers of the Regina Coeli environmentally safe apartments in Dallas where I lived for seven months, were kind in so many ways I dare not detail them for fear I would forget some of their kindnesses. Their son, Josh, now sadly deceased, was my main driver between the apartments and the clinic; our shared interest in classic cars provided much-needed distraction from the rigors of treatment.

I am immensely grateful to Dr. Leo Galland for his appraisal of my symptoms, as well as of the environment in our home, and for his recommendation that I seek treatment at the Environmental Health Center-Dallas (EHC-D). At the EHC-D, I owe my gratitude to a legion of people. To Dr. William J. Rea, founder and medical director, who exposed Roger and me to a different way of thinking about environmental toxins and health, I am deeply indebted. Dr. Rea's treatment approach provided the allopathic therapies that helped us both recover from environmental illness and led me, as well, to conquer the chronic illnesses with which I had been diagnosed. Dr. Rea is a man of great foresight and courage, who has had to stare down those who would discredit his ground-breaking work, as many pioneering clinicians in the past were forced to do. The sickest of the environmentally ill are referred to Dr. Rea from many countries, and his treatment methods help many regain normal functioning in a world that has become increasingly hostile to those with sensitivities. To the many people who worked at Dr. Rea's clinic while I was in treatment, including Trep Piamonte, Jayne Miller, Tim Rea, Estella Scaggs, Betty Bruce, Joseph

Martinez, Billie Whiteside, Mark Michalica, Florence Florez, Elena Contreras, Jennifer Rightsell, as well as those who worked at the American Environmental Health Foundation, especially Brenda Bryant, or in the antigen laboratory, especially Ina Kavandava, I send my heartfelt thanks for their compassion and patience.

My life changed when I met Deborah Singleton and her healing team. Deborah's approach to the human energy system, developed over many years, has transformed the lives and health of the many who have sought her help from all over the world. Those of us who have had the good fortune to come under her tutelage have benefited from her wisdom. Deborah is often described by the people who meet her as "extraordinary." Certainly, I can attest to that. Her infinite patience in allowing me to grow and develop as a spiritual being and to discover, on my own, my calling to help others was a gift that opened new worlds to me. I will always be grateful. My thanks go also to the exceptional team of healers who have worked—Elizabeth Ellison, Terri Ford, Christy Hart, Melanie Murray—or are working—Carol Cole, Judy Lyle, Mark Michalica, Laura Sarna—under Deborah's direction at A Healing Place. They have all been my teachers, and I am thankful for what they have shared with me. Growing with my fellow apprentices at A Healing Place—Susan McGraw, Alma Obinger, Barbara Tudhope—has been a privilege.

Dr. Carol Cole helped me to keep myself grounded in my relationships and guided me to new ways of thinking about illness and emotional health. She was one of my anchors while I was in treatment and for several years afterwards. Dr. Ron Overberg provided invaluable nutritional counseling while I was in treatment and afterwards.

To the people who walked my healing path with me after Roger and I moved to Santa Fe, I express deep gratitude. They include Christine Gregg, Dr. Erica Elliott, Jerome Bernstein, Maya Page, Larry Archie, Johnson Dennison, and Gerald King.

Their parts in my healing journey will be revealed as my story unfolds. Heartfelt thanks go also to Tsundue and Tsewang Tenzin and their children for their kindnesses to us while we were recovering in Santa Fe and afterwards for their enduring friendship. Finally, Sheila and Stu Millendorf made it possible for us to attend homeowners meetings in our community by requesting that members not wear scents when I was still acutely sensitive. I am grateful for their efforts and their friendship.

I owe a debt of gratitude to Marsha Scarbrough, author of *Medicine Dance: One woman's healing journey into the world of Native American sweatlodges, drumming meditations and dance fasts*, who introduced me to Tim Ward, a much-published author but also an acquisitions editor for O-Books at the time of our introduction. Tim is now my publisher as the director of the Changemakers Books imprint. Tim's insightful comments on my manuscript helped me to shape it for publication. I also thank the other people who read the numerous drafts of my manuscript, including Roger, Colin, Dr. Rea, Deborah Singleton, Dr. Cole, Dr. Elliott, Jerome Bernstein, Christine Gregg, Maya Page, and Marsha Scarbrough, as well as the readers and production staff at O-Books. Of course, if any errors appear in the text, they are solely mine.

INTRODUCTION

I lay in the darkness. The heat rising up from the bottom of the pit was intense, and I was drenched in sweat. I could hear the chanting of the medicine man, but the sound was muffled by the blankets covering the opening. The air in the pit was heavy and laced with the scent of steaming herbs, cedar, and spruce. I was coughing. A corner of the blankets was suddenly pulled back, and the medicine man thrust a gourd at me.

"Drink as much as you can."

I managed three large gulps of the bitter liquid and handed the gourd back. I lay back down and the pit was sealed once again. I started talking to Jesus.

How did I get here? How did a Catholic schoolgirl, whose education was punctuated with daily devotions to Jesus, Mary, and Joseph, wind up in a pit on the property of a medicine man in Navajo country?

From the time I was eighteen years old and throughout my adult life, symptoms related to chronic illnesses had sent me to the offices of specialists in New York, Maryland, Washington, D.C., and Louisiana. I was diagnosed with colitis and lactose intolerance by a physician at Staten Island Hospital in New York, reactive hypoglycemia by an internist at St. Joseph's Hospital in suburban Maryland, fibromyalgia by the then chief of rheumatology and immunology at Georgetown University Hospital in Washington, D.C., and gastro-esophageal reflux disease (GERD) by a gastroenterologist at East Jefferson General Hospital in Louisiana. These diagnoses were based on the results of tests and clinical examinations. I suffered from migraines, intense muscle pain, fatigue, constant yeast infections, esophageal burning, and sensitivities to medications. Many of the physicians I consulted considered me "sensitive." No one, however, could tell me why I was sensitive or exactly what it was that had triggered these sensitivities. Fibromyalgia, for instance, at the time of my diagnosis in 1990, was thought to be a condition whereby certain pathways of pain were activated. Specific triggers, however, had not been identified. Today, more than twenty years later, fibromyalgia is described in television commercials advertising new medications for this condition as "over-reactivity" of nerves, leading to chronic pain. This description, of course, is not much different from the one I was given in 1990. The new medications target the over-reactivity, but none goes beyond the symptoms to treat the *cause* of over-reactivity, which is still unknown in mainstream medicine.

When my husband, Roger, a physician and epidemiologist, and I arrived in New Orleans in January 1999, the symptoms of the chronic illnesses with which I had been diagnosed to that point were being controlled by a combination of prescription drugs (including hormone replacement therapy), exercise (I was an amateur ballroom dancer and a dedicated walker), and diet. Despite the best medical care, based on evidence from research studies, I still suffered from debilitating episodes of these illnesses, especially fibromyalgia. Yet, I considered myself fortunate that I could live the life of a twentieth century woman— wife, mother, and career woman—with the aid of the century's potent medications. While mainstream medical science could not tell me why I suffered from chronic illness, it could on the other hand medicate the symptoms that had made life difficult for me. This in no way implies criticism of mainstream medicine, which has increased our knowledge of how the body works and developed lifesaving vaccines as well as treatment for chronic conditions, such as cardiovascular disease and diabetes, surgical procedures that save lives, and devices that help people to function in the face of catastrophic injuries. As a public health writer and editor and the wife of a physician, I do not take a biased view of mainstream medicine. I have observed, in the course of my healing journey, however, that mainstream medicine does not seem to have recognized thus far the roots of the chronic illnesses that plagued me. I am a living example that recovery is possible after those roots have been identified and mitigated. How those roots were determined, which allopathic and complementary medical therapies helped me to recover, and the spiritual growth that led to my finding the healer within are the organizing themes for this book.

My healing journey began in New Orleans after chronic and acute exposure to type II pyrethroid pesticides triggered a host of debilitating symptoms. Finding no one in New Orleans who could advise me, I consulted Dr. Leo Galland in New York City. He, in turn, referred me to Dr. William J. Rea, founder and director of the Environmental Health Center-Dallas (EHC-D). Dr. Rea introduced me to the view held by doctors of environmental medicine that many chronic illnesses are triggered by environmental toxins. During the course of treatment at his clinic, I "unmasked" for electromagnetic field (EMF) sensitivity. Dr. Rea referred me to Deborah Singleton, founder and president of the Arasini Foundation, and her energy healing team, now in Richardson, Texas, at A Healing Place. Under their guidance I learned about the potential of healing from within. While the allopathic treatment program at the EHC-D helped to reduce my sensitivities to environmental toxins, what I learned from Deborah Singleton, as well as from Dr. Carol Cole, holistic psychotherapist, led me to accept that in order for my physical body to recover fully from environmental and other chronic illnesses, my emotional, mental, and most especially, my spiritual energy fields needed to heal.

For me, a public health writer and editor who, among other things, reported on best practices based on medical research, the most important decision I made after learning about the effects of chronic and acute exposure to toxic substances, was to be open to alternative and complementary medical therapies for which research trials are in their infancy. That decision led me to healing pathways I would never have contemplated as a conservative, Western-educated woman, taking me from energy medicine deep into the heart of the Navajo Nation and to healing from Navajo *hataałi*, or "singers."

My first encounters with energy healing triggered in me a process that continues to this day, a process that is called by many "awakening." It was awakening to who I really am and following guidance from within that helped me to cross the barrier between illness and wellness. Did I heal as a result of Dr. Rea's treatment program and the complementary medical therapies I sought and received? I most certainly did. The secret weapons in my medical armamentarium, however, were, first, faith—a belief from deep within myself that I would heal—and, second, openness to communication from the realm of the soul, the energetic world I began to recognize as I "awakened."

1 NEW ORLEANS

January 1999 to November 1999

Roger's appointment as chair of a new department of epidemiology at the Tulane University School of Public Health and Tropical Medicine had brought us to New Orleans shortly after our late-in-life marriage. An internist by training, Roger had pursued a career in medical research at both Johns Hopkins University and the University of Maryland School of Medicine in Baltimore. We married after a courtship that had begun in January 1996 while he was Professor of Medicine at UMD and I was Managing Editor of publications for a public health consulting firm in Chevy Chase.

Two weeks after our marriage we moved into the townhouse we had rented on Lake Pontchartrain, which had been renovated only two years earlier. Roger concentrated on setting up the new department, and I worked to get us settled in our new home. The plan was that I would telecommute for my employer, a Maryland-based consulting company, from a home office, which I did once my office was set up.

Pyrethroid Pesticides

One day during the second month we were living in New Orleans, I received a notice that exterminators would be treating our townhouse on a particular day. When the exterminators arrived, they explained that they treated all of the units regularly with a pesticide, a pyrethroid. Having never lived in a house in which the interior had been treated by exterminators, I was concerned about possible allergic effects given my sensitivities. I was told not to worry because the pesticide had "no effect on people and pets." Reassured, I dismissed my concerns.

Another Chronic Illness

About a month after the pesticide treatment, while taking a break from work at lunchtime, I remembered that I was to start taking medication that day for allergic symptoms, hives in particular, I had reported a week earlier to my new gynecologist. I walked into the kitchen, prepared something to eat, and took a tablet. All of a sudden I felt a ball of fire above my waist. The ball rushed up into my chest, causing crushing pain, which radiated down my left arm. I began to have trouble breathing. I thought I was having a heart attack. I sank into a chair and called 911. I blurted out the requested information, and emergency medical technicians (EMTs) were dispatched. Clutching my chest in agonizing pain, I managed a call to Roger. Luckily, he was at his desk.

"Roger, I may be having a heart attack. Burning pain in my chest and down my left arm."

"Have you called 911?"

"Yes."

"Tell the EMTs to take you to the Tulane emergency room. Have them call ahead. I'm on my way."

I could no longer speak. My throat and mouth were burning as if I had swallowed a boiling liquid. In the meantime, Roger rushed out of his office to his car and raced home in an attempt to beat the EMTs to our door. He was not successful. We finally met in the emergency room, where I was being tested for cardiac distress. When all of the cardiac tests yielded normal results, a physician came to talk to us.

"Your cardiac tests are all normal. Given your description of the symptoms you experienced, I suspect you had an esophageal spasm. I've ordered a cocktail of liquid medications. If it works and the pain calms down, my suspicions will be confirmed. I'll release you with a prescription and a referral to a gastroenterologist."

"An esophageal spasm?" I managed weakly.

"Yes. A sudden reflux of acid into the esophagus can make the esophagus twist away from the acid, so to speak, and it can push against the diaphragm."

"That's why it was hard to breathe?"

"Yes."

The cocktail worked. A week later I saw a gastroenterologist who, after performing a gastroscopy and a colonoscopy to rule out more serious conditions, told me that I had GERD, gastro-esophageal reflux disease. She asked me to follow a bland diet and to take one of the classes of medicines used to treat GERD. From March 1999 to October 2002 I would try several classes of medicine for GERD, each of which brought me only limited relief. There I was, living in one of the culinary centers of the United States, unable to eat the local specialties, and suffering from continual bouts of esophageal burning. And I still had hives! I reported my problem with the medication to my gynecologist, who of course told me to discontinue it. She suspected I might be allergic to the oral hormones I had been taking, so she asked me to try a hormone patch. The patch seemed to agree with me, and my hives subsided. I continued to see my gynecologist periodically for continuing vaginal yeast and other infections, which were chronic. She treated me as one of her "sensitive" patients, taking the precaution of using non-latex examination gloves.

The legion of women who suffer from periodic or chronic yeast infections know firsthand the symptoms associated with these illnesses—intense itching, burning, and pain upon urination. When they recur repeatedly, they markedly decrease a woman's quality of life. Intimacy is affected, as are relationships. There were many times throughout my adult life when I despaired of ever being without vulval pain and able to wear close-fitting clothing. I adhered to anti-yeast diets, took anti-fungal medications as directed, followed recommended cleansing routines, and went for regular examinations. Mainstream medicine offered me temporary symptomatic relief but could not explain to my satisfaction why I was caught in a cycle of infection and temporary recovery, followed by infection.

2 DOWNWARD SPIRAL

November 1999 to July 2002

In November 1999 we moved into a recently renovated condominium in the Central Business District that was within walking distance of the Vieux Carré (the French Quarter) and the Tulane medical campus. I served as secretary on the board of the condominium owners' association. I was not surprised to learn that our condos were treated periodically with pesticides, which I later found out were pyrethroids.

At Roger's suggestion, I resigned from my position with the consulting company. He had asked me to work with him on a book, as well as on grant proposals to bring research funds into the new department. Happy as I was to work with my husband, I was even happier to resign from the work I had been doing. The longer we lived in New Orleans, the sicker I became. I found it difficult to concentrate on the various projects assigned to me, while needing time to see all of the doctors to whom I had been referred about the symptoms I was experiencing. Luckily, I met and was able to establish a professional relationship with an internist at Tulane who had been voted one of the top 100 internists in the nation. He was incredibly patient, never dismissing any of my symptoms as being "all in my head." As each new symptom appeared, he referred me to the appropriate specialists. They included an allergist and a dermatologist for the hives and other allergic reactions I was having to medications, personal care products, and foods. While the allergist's tests did not detect sensitivities, a provocative skin-testing panel the dermatologist applied to my back revealed sensitivity to methylisothiazolinone, a chemical found in the face cream, skin lotion, other personal care products, and toilet tissue I had been using. When I asked how I could have become sensitive to this chemical, the dermatologist explained that the longer a person is exposed to any substance, the greater the likelihood that sensitivity to that substance will develop. The question he couldn't answer, of course, was: Of the millions of people using these same products, why do only a few, including me, become sensitive? Luckily for me, he was able to trace the hives, which had suddenly appeared again, to the Earl Grey tea I was drinking, by the pattern of the hives on my neck. When I stopped drinking the tea, which contains oil of bergamot, the substance to which I had become sensitive, the hives disappeared. Naturally, I was puzzled that I was becoming sensitive to more and more substances. Neither my husband nor the specialists I was seeing could explain what was happening to me. Yet, I continued to have faith that one of the specialists would find the key to the growing number of sensitivities I was developing. I was married to a physician, and we were part of a community that supported medical research. *Surely,* I thought, *someone will figure it out.*

Fibromyalgia Again

In the fall of 2001, shortly after competing in the Louisiana Regional Dancesport Championships, the fibromyalgia flared. The muscle pain became unbearable, and I had to stop dancing. I fought the pain with information. A friend with fibromyalgia gave me a book written by a physician in California who had been using high doses of guaifenesin to treat patients with fibromyalgia. My friend reported a miraculous remission of pain, as did the patients quoted in the book. With Roger's encouragement and a referral from our internist to a physician in Baton Rouge who was using the guaifenesin protocol, I tried this non-mainstream medical treatment. Guaifenesin, according to the author of the book, works by drawing an overload of phosphates (which he identified as one of the underlying causes of the muscle pain) out of the cells for release through the kidneys. The first buildup of phosphates in the tissues causes considerable pain. In my case the pain was so bad that I found it difficult to walk. Eventually, the pain decreased, but by the time that happened, I could not go back to dance because of my growing sensitivities to the personal care products worn by other dancers. My sensitivity to colognes and hairspray had become so pronounced that I could not breathe easily when exposed to them. Dance had been one of the tools I had used to ward off fibromyalgia flares, and I had lost it. *How will I cope?* I asked myself. I wasn't sure.

Hormone Sensitivity

At the beginning of 2002 I became sensitive to the hormone patch I had been wearing since 1999. The initial symptoms included shakiness and mild anxiety. They were followed by insomnia with severe anxiety. Roger suggested I cut the patch in half to lessen the side effects. The half became a quarter, then an eighth, and finally a thirty-second. Giving up, I stopped taking hormones altogether, despite continuing menopausal symptoms and the concern that the fibromyalgia symptoms would flare again. Day after day, I walked an hour in the mornings and an hour in the evenings in the hope of heading off a major relapse. And I started to do something I hadn't done in years. I prayed. *Jesus, Blessed Mother Mary, I ask you both for help.* I felt like a hypocrite. I had turned away from my childhood faith many years prior, but I was desperate. I said "Hail Marys" and "Our Fathers" in a familiar sequence, praying a rosary in my head. I walked through the discomfort in my muscles and the heat of New Orleans with tears in my eyes. When I reached the point of nearly total despair, my prayers were answered, but not in the way I had expected.

3 CRISIS

July 2002 to October 2002

In July 2002 the lobby of our building was ravaged by termites, and our kitchen was invaded by an army of weevils. The management company of our condominium association called in an exterminator to treat the lobby with pesticides. I called in an exterminator to treat our kitchen cabinets. On the morning of August 2 as I was waiting for the exterminators, Annie Jackson, who ran her own housekeeping business, came in to help me with chores I was not able to manage because of the fibromyalgia pain. A little while later the exterminators, an older man who appeared to be in charge and a younger man, arrived with spray cans and hoses. I showed the men the cabinets, now empty except for weevils. "Can you explain what you're going to do?"

The older man answered: "I'm going to spray the cabinets with a liquid pyrethroid, and my partner will inject a powdered form of the pesticide into the wall behind the cabinets." Seeing the look of concern on my face, he added: "Don't worry. Pyrethroids have no effects on people and pets."

Still, given my recent reactions to personal care products, I packed my bag to leave. In the meantime, the men, anxious to get on, started to work. Suddenly, as I was talking to Annie, I felt red-hot burning in my scalp, which quickly spread to the rest of my body. I recognized immediately that I was reacting to a chemical. Earlier in the year I had had a similar reaction to color my hairdresser was applying to my hair and had asked him to wash it out within seconds of his applying it. I started shaking and felt intense pressure in my chest, making breathing difficult. I screamed, and one of the men told me to run out. I grabbed my bag and fled. I did not have the presence of mind, under the circumstances, to tell the men to stop working or to ask Annie to come with me. I sat outside shaking, thinking I was about to stop breathing. I don't know how long I sat there. Eventually, I remembered that Roger was out of town at a medical meeting in Denver and I had a lunch date with our friend Kelly, who was also a colleague of my husband. When I could breathe more easily, I called her. Shaking, I explained what had happened. She asked me to come to the medical campus, promising to go with me to see our internist. I called home to speak to Annie, who reported no symptoms. She said she would finish up and let herself out. The men, in the meantime, had completed their work and gone. By the time I arrived on the medical campus, the shaking and burning had stopped and I was breathing more easily. Kelly suggested we have something to eat, and we walked to a restaurant across from Roger's office on the Tulane Medical campus. Our internist was just finishing his lunch. He recommended that I not return to our condo for the weekend and that I get someone to open the windows to air out our kitchen. After eating lunch, I returned to the office with Kelly to await Roger's return that afternoon.

When Roger arrived, he decided that he would go into our apartment to the kitchen to open the windows, while I went directly into our bedroom, which was in an area accessible from the front door and away from the kitchen. The plan was that I would avoid the kitchen until the effects of the pesticides dissipated, which we hoped would happen overnight. Annie called to see how I was. She agreed to come back the next morning to wash down the cabinets that had been sprayed.

Cleanup Accident

The next morning I went into the kitchen to prepare breakfast. No sooner had I entered than I started shaking from head to toe. I ran back to the bedroom, once again unable to think clearly, experiencing chest pain and breathing with difficulty. Annie arrived to wash down the cabinets, reporting that she had had a headache the night before but other than that she was feeling fine. Roger suggested we call the exterminators to ask them to remove the pesticide that had been inserted into the kitchen wall. When I reached one of the exterminators, he said they did not do removal work, and we would have to remove the pesticide ourselves. "Tell your husband to take off the electrical outlet covers and insert the small nozzle of your vacuum cleaner hose into the outlet."

I relayed the instructions to Roger who dutifully complied. What the exterminator had failed to explain, however, was that in order to remove pesticide dust with a vacuum cleaner safely, the cleaner must be equipped with a high-efficiency particulate air (HEPA) filter. Ours was not. When Roger switched on the vacuum cleaner, the cleaner sucked up the pesticide dust and exhausted it into the room. "Oops," my English born and bred husband said, as the dust seeped into our air conditioning ducts. I ran to the control panel for the air conditioning system and shut down the system. We retreated to the other side of the condominium to regroup. Roger and Annie appeared to be unaffected by the pesticide exposure. I was, once again, shaking from head to toe. Annie left. We sat in silence on the sofa in my home office. The look on Roger's face was one of total dismay. *We made it worse*, I thought. *How is it that two intelligent people know so little about cleaning up pesticides?* I felt defeated.

We found ourselves living in our bedroom with the air conditioning turned off in 98-degree heat. I was unable to enter the other rooms of our condominium without risking a recurrence of symptoms that included chest pain, difficulty breathing, head-to-toe tremors, and rapid heartbeat. Roger became alarmed at the neurological symptoms I began to exhibit the longer we lived in our home. I found it difficult to carry on conversations because I was unable to retrieve words from my memory to express a thought. Roger would say something to me, and a minute later I would forget what he had said. We started to argue over the content of our conversations. When Roger started writing down what he had said to me so I wouldn't forget, I suddenly realized that something was wrong. *Is this how it feels when someone develops Alzheimer's?* I asked myself. I would not let myself dwell on that thought.

While we were waiting for an environmental cleanup company to schedule a cleanout of the pesticides in our condominium, I looked, albeit with great difficulty because of my inability to concentrate, for an apartment or a hotel room to rent. What I discovered was that pyrethroids, specifically type II pyrethroids, are used in houses, apartments, hotels, and other buildings throughout New Orleans. The pesticide to which we had been exposed acutely in our condominium was the same type of pesticide to which we had been exposed chronically during the four years we had been living in New Orleans. There was nowhere safer for us to live than in our bedroom with the air conditioning turned off.

No Help

In the meantime, normal life for us came to an end. Social engagements were cancelled. My sensitivity to cologne and hairspray worsened. My throat would tighten, I would have difficulty breathing, and my heart would race whenever I was near a scented person. The spraying of glass cleaner would elicit the same response. It seemed that no matter where I went, I would encounter unseen substances that would trigger asthma attacks, rapid heartbeat, tremors, and worse. A trip to a hair salon for a manicure sent me by ambulance to Tulane's emergency room. Our internist referred me to a neurologist and to a pulmonary specialist who was board-certified as a pulmonolgist and an allergist. Neither could explain the symptoms I was having, although the pulmonologist/allergist told me I had reduced lung capacity. She prescribed steroids for me. I did not fill the prescription. Our dermatologist had warned me against using steroids after I had had an atypical reaction to one he had prescribed. The neurologist, who told me upon my entering his office that he had no knowledge of symptoms related to pesticide exposure, suggested I consult a psychiatrist. When I told Roger what the neurologist had recommended, he exploded. "He doesn't know what is wrong, and he is implying that what is wrong is all in your head! Unacceptable!"

I, too, was dismayed by the neurologist's attitude toward me. For me, however, it was nothing new. I had encountered similar reactions from physicians I had consulted when I first started having symptoms that were eventually diagnosed as symptoms of fibromyalgia. I knew, too, that fibromyalgia was considered by some in the medical establishment to be a "waste-basket" diagnosis for an array of symptoms no one could explain. Although this assessment infuriated me at the time, later I would come to agree with it, but for very different reasons than the ones held by the medical establishment.

New Jersey

Finally, the day arrived for the cleanout of our condominium, and I flew to New Jersey to visit my parents. The cleaners had recommended I not be home for at least a week after the cleanout. I had briefed my parents on the problems I was having so they did their best to create a non-reactive environment for me before I arrived. Nevertheless, I noticed scents in their home I had never noticed before. I could barely stand to be near the gas stove (the smell of gas was so strong), and the scent of their laundry detergent was suddenly intense. I accompanied my mother on a visit to a friend's house. I had to sit by an open window because the smell of the air freshener in the friend's house overwhelmed me, causing my throat to tighten. Despite what was happening to me, I attempted to make the visit as pleasant as possible. Because one of my mother's favorite pastimes was shopping, I drove her to a new clothing outlet and walked inside with her to look around. Within minutes of entering, I was assaulted by symptoms similar to those I had experienced when our kitchen in New Orleans was being treated with pesticides. I ran outside and looked for a place to sit down, while shaking, trembling, feeling my throat tighten, breathing with difficulty, and experiencing a sensory overload that was causing anxiety.

First Hope

While I was staying with my parents, I was referred to Dr. Leo Galland in New York City by a woman who had been under his care for pesticide exposure and had recovered. I called for an appointment and was lucky to obtain one through a last-minute cancellation. After a thorough history and examination, Dr. Galland explained that the symptoms I reported to him were symptoms of chronic and acute exposure to pesticides. The cascade of symptoms I had endured in New Orleans was now being linked to pesticides. *Could the other illnesses and sensitivities that had.made life so difficult for me as an adult be linked to pesticides as well?* I began to wonder. Dr. Galland outlined an approach for testing and treatment. He advised me to return home to see if I could tolerate our condominium after the cleanout. He cautioned me that since I had become sensitized I might not be able to tolerate even minute amounts of the pesticides that had been used. He told me then that should I fail to tolerate the environment in our home, my only hope for recovery was to enter into sauna detoxification treatment at Dr. William J. Rea's clinic, called the Environmental Health Center-Dallas, in Texas. Two weeks later I returned home. Within one week of returning, I bought a one-way ticket to Dallas.

4 DALLAS

October 2002

I arrived in Dallas on Sunday, October 14, 2002, with a carry-on suitcase purchased for the trip and filled with new clothes I had bought and stored in our car. The new-patient advisor at Dr. Rea's clinic had cautioned me not to bring anything from our home. I took a taxi from the airport to the environmentally safe apartment I was to stay in while I was in treatment. I paid the driver, walked into the courtyard, and stood there looking around. I had never seen a bleaker environment. Grey stone buildings surrounded the dusty courtyard. They seemed to compete for air and space with the few blades of grass that bravely poked up from beneath the arid soil. I was so filled with dread at the thought of living in those drab Dallas apartments, even temporarily, that I immediately thought of leaving. At that moment, a voice called out to me, and I turned to see who was speaking. A woman was seated on the ground outside one of the apartments wearing a thick, white mask, the sight of which startled me. "Hi," she said. "I'm Susi. Are you checking in?"

"I am."

"Where are you from?"

"New Orleans. My name is Jennie."

"Hi, Jennie. Come with me," Susi said. "I'll show you where the manager's office is."

I found a note and a key for the apartment assigned to me. I let myself into the apartment and walked around. Within minutes, I was shaking uncontrollably and having difficulty breathing. I fled the apartment and looked for Susi. She was still seated on the ground outside her apartment.

"Susi, hi again. There is something wrong with that apartment."

"You couldn't tolerate it?"

"I guess not."

"Several people have left that apartment," she explained.

"Why is that?"

"Some of them suspected mold. Follow me. Let's go to Beverly's apartment. I can't use a telephone, but Beverly can and maybe she can make some phone calls for you."

I couldn't think of anything to say, although several questions raced through my mind. *You can't use a phone? Why not? What is it that prevents you from using a telephone?* I said nothing. I didn't want to pry.

When we got to Beverly's apartment, Susi knocked. A tall man with a large shock of dark hair answered the door.

"Hi, Dick. Can we speak to Beverly?" Dick invited us in.

"Hi, Susi."

I looked across the room and saw a petite attractive woman. She greeted us with a smile. Susi introduced me and explained why we had come.

"It's nice to meet you, Jennie. Have you been traveling all day?"

"Since breakfast." I looked at my watch. It was now four o'clock in the afternoon.

"You must be hungry. Do you know your sensitivities?"

"To foods? Dairy, fruit, and foods containing sugar."

"Would you like a glass of spring water and a yeast-free bagel?" I accepted gratefully.

After I had eaten, Beverly took me to see the resident assistant manager, who explained that all of the other apartments were occupied.

"Let's call the Remmels," Beverly said. "They have safe apartments, too."

As luck would have it, an apartment was available, and Beverly asked Dick to drive me over to see the apartment. I said goodbye to Beverly and drove with Dick to the Greenville section of Dallas. I took out my cell phone and called Roger to let him know I had arrived safely but might be returning home if I could not find an apartment I could tolerate.

Safe Haven

When we arrived at the Remmels' apartment complex, called *Regina Coeli,* Dick told me I would find Earl Remmel near apartment 107. I found my way to 107. There I met Earl, a trim-looking man who appeared to be about my age, and his son, Josh, who I found out later was a year older than my son. After I told Earl what had happened at the other apartment, he invited me to sit inside apartment 104 for awhile. I opened the door to 104 and found a three-hundred-square-foot one-bedroom apartment with tile floors. There was a glass and metal table with metal chairs in the dining area adjacent to the galley kitchen and a bed of light-colored wood I couldn't identify in the bedroom. I felt a sort of buzz when I was near the bed, but I could breathe easily. I walked into the living room, which had a television, a sofa, and a phone. I sat down and glanced at the entry door. Hanging above it was a crucifix. I rubbed my eyes. The crucifix was still there. Were my prayers being answered? Suddenly, I had a strong feeling that divine intervention had brought me to Dallas. I decided I would stay, even though I knew I was reacting to something in the bedroom. I couldn't tell what it was, but my reactions were mild compared to those I had experienced earlier. I told Earl I would stay. I walked to Whole Foods Market®, which was nearby, and bought what I needed for the next few days. That night I thought over the events of the day. I remembered Susi, who could not be outside unless she wore a mask and could not use a telephone. I was terrified. What kind of a world was I entering? I picked up my cell phone and called Roger to tell him all that had transpired since my earlier call. I checked e-mail on my laptop, watched television for a while, and went to bed.

The Clinic

When I got to the clinic the next day, I learned more about the world I had entered, the world of environmental illness (EI). First of all, I had to turn off my cell phone, which annoyed me. Second, everything inside the clinic was made of porcelain, steel, or glass. The rooms looked and felt cold to me. The lack of warmth notwithstanding, I was able to breathe comfortably, and for that I was grateful. I would learn later that all the materials used in the clinic's rooms were chosen to minimize the reactivity of the most sensitive patients. I would come to appreciate those materials the longer I remained in treatment at the clinic. Many patients were wearing masks inside the building; some were taking oxygen. *Oh, Lord,* I thought, *what am I doing here? How did everyone get so sick? Does anyone ever get better? Be quiet,* I admonished myself. *You're here because you can't breathe when someone sprays glass cleaner. You can't be near anyone wearing cologne. You can't see your doctors because you shake from head to toe when you sit in the waiting room, and no one knows why. You've had to stop eating many foods because of esophageal burning. You've had to stop using many personal care products because of allergic reactions. You can't go out anywhere without risking asthma attacks and tachycardia. You can't think clearly. You can't work. You can't lead a normal life. If you can't be helped here, where else can you go?*

I met with the new-patient advisor, turned in all of the forms I had filled out, and took my seat in the waiting room. I looked at the other people seated there and watched as staff and patients, most of whom were women, walked through to the testing area. I made a mental note to ask why so many more women than men were patients, and I continued to look around. As a writer, I tend to observe people carefully—how they dress, how they speak, how they move their bodies. What I saw did not encourage me. The pallor of the patients' faces lent a ghostly air to their appearance. They seemed only half-materialized shadows, a phenomenon I would come to know very well the longer I lived in this world. It was not just that they looked ill. They seemed to wear an aura of apartness, a cloak that I would understand later all EI patients adopt in self-defense, with avoidance and, ultimately, survival as their goals.

I looked closely at a teenage girl who had paused on her way into the treatment area. She appeared to be about the age of the students I had taught years earlier, before my career in public health consulting, and, in fact, reminded me of a bright young woman who had been in one of my English classes. Although I was attracted by her liveliness, it was her clothing that held my rapt attention—sweatpants, a sweatshirt, and socks that seemed to have no discernible color. I would find out later, when I purchased the shorts and tops worn in the clinic's saunas, that my impressions had been correct. She had been wearing clothing made of organic cotton that was free of dyes, to which she and many other patients were exquisitely sensitive.

Dr. Rea

When I met Dr. Rea, I was surprised to find someone who seemed to know all about me. With every question he asked during the initial interview, he showed he understood what was wrong with me. I asked him how I could have become allergic to nearly everything in my environment. He patiently explained what I suspect he had explained to thousands of other patients before me—that I had become a universal reactor because of chronic exposure to toxins. The pesticide accident in our home was the final contribution to my tolerance limit, thought of as a barrel that overflows after its capacity has been reached. I asked if what I had been observing about the patient population was true, namely, that the majority of patients are women. Dr. Rea confirmed my observation, explaining that toxins bind with estrogens and are stored in fat cells. I recalled reading on the Internet about bioenvironmental research on certain environmental toxins, called "estrogen disruptors," which were found to bind with estrogens. Although researchers were not willing to make connections between these toxins and illness because the research was ongoing, practitioners who treat environmental illness already had. Knowing that observations made by practitioners of medicine often, after years of resistance, are absorbed into the sanctioned body of medical knowledge, I was more than willing to accept the connection between the exposure to toxins and the development of illness. Further, since women have by natural constitution more fat cells and a greater quantity of estrogens in their bodies, I understood how they could be more vulnerable, in general, to toxins than men.

We explored my medical history. I outlined for Dr. Rea the diagnoses I had received to that point in my life as well as the symptoms from which I had suffered—migraines, intense muscle pain, esophageal spasms and burning, hives, and constant yeast infections. I explained that the symptoms that had brought me to his clinic, however, had begun recently and included severe reactive asthma, tachycardia, and periodic mild dysphasia, or the inability to express ideas, as well as short-term memory loss. Without hesitation, Dr. Rea told me that most of my symptoms were related to toxic exposures. The plan was to determine which toxins were setting off the symptoms and begin treatment. Once the treatment program worked, I could stop taking my medications. I could become completely well. I remember telling Dr. Rea that I would never give up my meds for fibromyalgia—that they were enabling me to live without daily debilitating pain. Months later, when I reported to Dr. Rea that I had, in fact, given up those medications, he reminded me of what I had said.

5 TREATMENT

October 2002 to November 2002

The next day I continued my education at the clinic. I found out that the makeup and nail polish I was wearing contained toxic substances. I realized I would have to go without both in order to detox successfully. Having grown up thinking a woman wasn't dressed without makeup, not wearing it made me feel less feminine and a bit naked. I rationalized that I'd have to pack fewer things for my daily saunas at the clinic. Another rude surprise awaited me. During my day two consultation with Dr. Rea, he recommended I wear a mask while outside and advised me not to walk outdoors for exercise, since the air in Dallas is highly polluted. I had been walking an hour or two a day for years to mitigate the pain of fibromyalgia. While in treatment, however, I had to give up outdoor exercise to avoid "putting back into my body," as Dr. Rea had said, "what the treatment was helping to remove."

First Sauna

I reported to the sauna therapy area for my first sauna and met Jayne Miller. A massage therapist with special training to oversee sauna depuration, Jayne seemed to be everywhere at once. Her boundless energy stood out in high relief to the lethargy of the patients at the clinic. At that moment, I wanted to be like Jayne — well and, above all else, cheerful.

"Jennie Sherwin, nice to meet you," she boomed at me.

Really, I thought to myself, *even her voice has life.*

"First time in the sauna, right?"

"Yes."

"Do you have a prescription?"

"I do." I handed it over.

"Your first sauna will be timed for fifteen minutes. As soon as the fifteen minutes are up, go right into the shower. There are non-toxic, fragrance-free shampoos and soaps in the shower. Make sure to shampoo your hair. Let me show you the shower room and the dressing area."

We walked past exercise equipment to a curtained area. Behind the curtain were two doors. One led to the shower and the other to the bathroom/dressing area, which had lockers.

"Store your things in a locker. Take off anything metal. Did you bring sauna clothes?"

"I did."

"Okay. When you're ready, come outside. I'll take your vital signs and give you supplements."

I undressed and stored my street clothes in a locker. I took off my jewelry and stuffed it into my purse. I pulled on the sauna clothes—colorless shorts, tee shirt, and socks. I glanced in the mirror as I walked out to Jayne's desk. The sauna clothes showed how thin I had gotten in New Orleans. I had done some fashion modeling in my twenties. *Thin enough to model again,* I thought. But the dark circles under my eyes betrayed me.

Jayne offered me an array of supplements and a mug of water with bi-salts (calcium carbonate and potassium bicarbonate) to bring into the sauna with me.

"Sip the water while you are in the sauna. When you finish it, wave to me, and I'll bring you another mug. Which exercise equipment would you like to use?"

I looked at the equipment. Years of living with the pain of fibromyalgia had sworn me off of all exercise equipment. I walked and I danced for exercise.

"Can I dance?"

"Sure. But where?"

"I'll dance around the equipment to start. What's in that other area?" I pointed to a short hallway to one side of the treadmill.

"That leads to the massage room. We recommend a massage after sauna."

"Do I have to have a massage?"

"You don't."

"I'll think about it."

I danced cha-cha and rumba steps around the stationary bicycles and step machines. After several minutes, I was ushered into a ceramic sauna.

"Can you see the clock?"

"Yes."

"Come out in fifteen minutes. I'll be tracking your time as well."

Jayne handed me a towel to sit on. "Thanks."

I sat down with my mug of water and dutifully sipped as instructed earlier. I felt the dry heat, which seemed to get hotter as the minutes passed. *Why am I not perspiring? Ugh, I am baking. Any hotter in here and I will explode!* Just as the clock showed my time was up, Jayne motioned for me to come out.

"Towels are on that shelf. Come over to my desk after you are dressed."

I found out later that it is common for EI patients not to perspire in sauna initially. Over the next week, my time in the sauna would be increased gradually until I was regularly taking 140-degree saunas of thirty minutes' duration, still without perspiring noticeably. I left the sauna area without having a massage. I knew I couldn't stand that much pressure on my muscles. I walked to the other end of the clinic to the American Environmental Health Foundation store. I bought a copy of *Rotational Bon Appetit,* a book which explains the four-day organic rotational diet that Dr. Rea recommends to his patients. Over the next few days I became familiar with the principles of the diet. Then I developed my own rotational diet plan, which was limited by my sensitivities to dairy, fruit, and foods containing sugar. For years, I had avoided those food items in an effort to keep the symptoms of lactose intolerance, chronic yeast infections, and reactive hypoglycemia under control.

Testing

On day three, having been cleared for testing, I reported to testing room A and discovered some of the differences between testing at the EHC-D and testing at an allergist's office. An allergist tests for simple yes or no sensitivity, using standard doses of allergens. At the EHC-D, patients are tested using a serial dilution approach that provides a measure of the patient's sensitivity. Neutralizing antigens can therefore be tailor-made in a dose appropriate to the individual. Another important difference is that the allergens used by allergists generally contain preservatives. At the EHC-D allergens are diluted with saline and contain no other preservatives to safeguard against a patient's reacting to the preservative and not to the allergen itself. For this reason, testing begins with determining a patient's reactivity to saline to rule out saline sensitivity. The testing rooms are kept quite cool, and wearing an easily removed sweater is advisable for long testing stretches.

I began the routine of skin testing that quickly becomes familiar to patients at the clinic. A tester injects a "05/1" dilution of the substance to be tested under the first two layers of skin on the patient's upper arm. The patient keeps track over a ten-minute period of any symptoms and waits to see if a wheal appears. If a wheal does appear, then the tester injects a "05/2" dilution, which is a measure weaker than the "05/1" dilution. If after ten minutes the patient has no wheal at the second injection site and no symptoms, the 05/2 dilution is the neutralizing endpoint for that substance. If, however, a wheal does appear at the second site, the tester injects a "05/3" dilution, and so on, in sequentially higher dilutions until the patient's endpoint is determined—the higher the dilution, the greater the sensitivity. The wheals are marked with washable ink, and the patient develops a telltale testing "tattoo."

One of the first substances I tested was poplar. There was something in the bedroom at the apartment to which I was reacting. Earl had told me the bed frame was made of poplar. Sure enough, I was sensitive to poplar. That evening I asked Earl to remove the bed. Since there was no other bed available, I asked him to put the mattress on the floor. With the bed gone, I was comfortable in the apartment. I called Roger.

"Earl removed the bed frame today. I tested sensitive to poplar, so I asked him to take it out of the apartment. Do you mind?"

"Is there another bed frame?"

"Earl said there is no other at the moment."

"If removing the bed frame helps you feel better, that's okay with me."

"You don't mind sleeping on a mattress on the floor?"

"I'll manage. Did I tell you that one of my MPH students loaned me volume one of Dr. Rea's textbook on chemical sensitivity?"

"No, but I'd like to know what you think of it."

"I'll let you know when I've finished reading it."

It was on day four that I experienced the first of many severe asthmatic reactions to substances I was testing. It had been my bad luck not to be able to find suitable endpoints for histamine and serotonin antigens, which are used to neutralize a reaction. Eventually, I learned to observe what was going on in my body and to recognize when my small airways had reached their limits for testing that day. This took time, however, and during the first few weeks my testing sessions often ended precipitously, with me in agonizing pain receiving oxygen therapy.

Roger's First Visit

I made it through the first week and was very happy to see Roger when he arrived on Saturday. The plan he had worked out with his Dean was that he would spend a week with me and then return to New Orleans for two weeks, then come back to Dallas for a week, and so on. We were very grateful to his Dean at the time and her successor for the understanding both showed us during my treatment and recovery. In fact, we were grateful to all of Roger's colleagues for their concern, in particular our friend Kelly and Roger's secretary, Wendy, whose support was invaluable to us.

Roger came with me to my next consultation with Dr. Rea. After reading volume one of Dr. Rea's textbook on chemical sensitivity, which he had found impressive, he decided to share it with a colleague who was a professor of biochemistry. His colleague had judged the biochemistry in the textbook sound, confirming Roger's opinion. Dr. Rea reviewed my case with us, discussing the results of tests I had had during the first week. He warned Roger that by the time I finished treatment I would probably be an environmental activist. We all laughed, but that is exactly what happened. Dr. Rea repeated to Roger what he had told me during my first consultation with him, namely, that I would become well again. He couldn't predict how long that would take, but he was sure I would be well again. Roger would remind me of Dr. Rea's conviction from time to time, especially when I was in periods of intense detoxification.

The routine we established during Roger's first visit to Dallas we maintained throughout each of his visits during my stay there. He would drive me to the clinic in the morning and return to the apartment to work. At lunchtime he would bring lunch to the clinic so we could eat together. Then he'd return to the apartment to work, picking me up at the end of the day. At the time I started treatment, Roger was seventy-one years old. Yet, every third week he would drive from New Orleans to Dallas so we could be together for a week (and back again to New Orleans at the end of the visit). When he knocked at the apartment door, I would greet him with a large plastic bag. He would step inside the door, strip off his clothes and put them into the bag, and then head straight for the bathtub. It was only after he had bathed that we could greet each other with a kiss and a hug. Because Roger was living in our condominium and being exposed to pesticides wherever he went in New Orleans, Dr. Rea had recommended this procedure to minimize exposure to me while in treatment. Roger willingly cooperated. Although each of us has an inner core of strength we can draw upon in adversity, I know my journey toward healing would have been much more difficult without my husband's support.

Sauna Downside

During the second week of treatment I started noticing that my sense of smell had gotten even stronger than it had been in New Orleans. I could smell scents people had been wearing long after they had passed by. This was not a particularly welcome new-found skill. Being anywhere near even lightly scented people became unbearable. Moreover, if their scent lingered on my clothing, I would have to wash those items of clothing several times in order to be able to wear them again. It was also during this second week that I started to perspire in the sauna. When that happened, I began experiencing symptoms as well. Sometimes I became nauseated; other times I would shake as if I were being exposed to toxins. Dr. Rea explained that I was beginning to "detox," and as that continued I would experience more symptoms. I remember shaking from head to toe the first time I removed my sweaty sauna clothes from my carry-all and realizing I was reacting to the clothes. After that, I started to pack a plastic bag for the used sauna clothes so that I would not have to touch them before washing them. Rather than discouraging me, my reaction to the sweaty clothing provided empirical evidence that the sauna detoxification treatment was helping me to shed toxic substances. The second week came to a close, and Roger returned to New Orleans.

6 EMF SENSITIVITY

Early November 2002

During my third week at the clinic, I saw two specialists to whom Dr. Rea had referred me for testing and consultation, and I continued skin testing and sauna detoxification. In addition to learning that naturally occurring substances in the environment, such as pollens and molds, can be toxic to many people, I was beginning to understand what it means to be a universal reactor. I was testing sensitive for molds, trees, grasses, weeds, IV nutrients (vitamins, minerals, and amino acids), cologne, chemicals, foods, and so on. Throughout this third week, however, I was becoming sicker and sicker during skin testing and sauna and had to continue taking oxygen therapy for reactions. The substances that precipitated the most violent reactions were minerals. After analysis of hair and red blood cells revealed that I was deficient in certain minerals, I began testing to determine which mineral supplements I could tolerate. I began with magnesium chloride and immediately regretted my decision. I had a nearly instantaneous reaction, an asthma episode that was so painful I could not ask for help. My reaction, however, was noticed immediately, and I was given oxygen. Further testing, of course, was suspended for the day. The next day, I returned to test magnesium sulfate, and the drama of the previous day repeated itself. This would continue until I had finished testing the minerals. At the end of each day, I was exhausted physically, mentally, and emotionally. It seemed that my chest would never stop hurting. After a particularly bad testing day, I called Roger.

"I don't think I can stand more of the treatment here. Coming to the clinic was a mistake. I am getting worse and not better. I want to leave."

"I have great confidence in Dr. Rea's treatment approach,"

Roger responded. "Weren't you told the course of treatment would be at least six weeks?"

"Yes."

"You haven't given the program a fair trial. Can you persevere through the sixth week?"

I respected Roger's opinions and instincts, so I reluctantly agreed. *It can't get worse, right?* I gamely encouraged myself.

A New Perception

The third week came to a close, and I prepared to spend the weekend alone, resting in the apartment. On Sunday early evening, as I was checking e-mail on my laptop, *Pretty Woman* was playing on one of the cable TV channels, and dinner was baking in the oven. All of a sudden, as I was typing, I felt a strange sensation. My fingers felt prickly. The sensation spread into my hands and up my arms. The next thing I knew waves of pain exploded in my chest, and I started shaking. I felt as if I had my finger in an electrical outlet and waves of electricity were coursing through my body. Electricity! That was it! I shut off the television, the computer, the oven, and all of the overhead lights. I sat in the dark, shaking, wondering if I was experiencing electromagnetic field (EMF) sensitivity. Remember Susi who couldn't use a telephone? She was EMF-sensitive, and for that reason she could not be near a telephone or other devices that emitted electromagnetic fields for very long. My third week at the clinic had ended, and I found myself much sicker than when I had arrived. I was incredulous. *It has gotten worse.* I looked at the telephone and took a deep breath. *Will I be able to use the phone?* Tomorrow morning, Roger would call me, and I would know.

The phone rang at six sharp, and I ran to pick it up. "Morning, Roger."

"Morning, Jennie."

I struggled to maintain my composure as I explained what had taken place the night before. I didn't get far. Electricity started crackling in my left hand, the hand with which I was holding the phone. It coursed up my arm and exploded in my chest.

"Rog, I'm so sorry. I need to get off the phone. Can you call me at the usual time?"

I had no idea how I would manage the phone later on. I just knew I had to stop the pain. Maybe, someone at the clinic would help me.

When I arrived at the clinic, I was told I had "unmasked" for EMF sensitivity as a result of the detoxification process that had been triggered in my body. "Unmasking" refers to the sudden emergence of a sensitivity of which one had been unaware. As the body clears itself of overriding sensitivities, it then recognizes or becomes conscious of underlying sensitivities. I was referred to the energy medicine healers at the Arasini Foundation, but I was not able to use a telephone to call for an appointment. The new-patient advisor made the call for me and put me on speaker phone. Standing about seven feet away from the phone, I was able to converse with someone at the Foundation. I was told that my name would be placed on a waiting list, and when an opening occurred, someone would call the clinic to let me know.

I had now entered a smaller segment of the EI world. I discovered, at the time, in a paper reporting research conducted at the University of Surrey, that about two percent of people with EI also develop EMF sensitivity. Years later, in June 2010, I would attend a symposium on EMF sensitivity, sponsored by the University of North Texas Health Science Center, Office of Professional and Continuing Education, and the American Environmental Health Foundation. Presenters reported that the incidence had changed. Now, thirty percent of people with EI also develop EMF sensitivity. In a world blanketed by WiFi and increasing numbers of cell phone towers, more people were becoming aware of, and affected by, electromagnetic fields.

Coming to Terms

People with EMF sensitivity live in a twilight zone, avoiding at every turn the electromagnetic fields that surround us. Electrical appliances and wires, transformers, telephones, computers, lights, cell phones, cell phone towers, airport security screeners, each of these can set off a painful reaction in an EMF-sensitive person. No two EMF-sensitive people, however, react to the same things. Each one learns through trial and error what to avoid. I learned quickly to avoid telephones, cell phones, computers, televisions, most overhead lights, the oven and the refrigerator in the apartment, the washing machines and dryers in the laundry room, my hair dryer and hair iron, and the HEPA air cleaners at the clinic and in the apartment.

I now had to learn to live in an even smaller world. Communication was my first consideration. I could tolerate a four-minute conversation on the telephone before the pain in my arms and chest would start, so Roger and I agreed upon the times for a morning and evening call, 6:00 a.m. and 6:00 p.m. I kept a notebook with me and jotted down things that I thought he would want to know. At the appointed time, he would call, and I would rattle off my list. Sometimes he had time to respond, other times we'd have to wait until the next conversation. He called my son, Colin, other family members, and friends to let them know I could no longer comfortably use a phone or a computer. I can't imagine what they all thought initially. I had not heard of EMF sensitivity before coming to Dallas, and if I had, most likely I would have dismissed it as the imaginings of the hysterical. Yet, there I was, experiencing it firsthand. Being cut off from my family and friends was extremely painful. At a time when I needed their love and support most, I could not speak to them by telephone or exchange e-mails. I took to writing letters in longhand, something I had not done in years.

The second consideration was cooking. I remembered the system I had used when Colin was in high school, living at home, and I was working full-time. Every weekend I would cook meals and freeze them for heating and eating during the week. I did the same thing while at the clinic, with a few EMF protective approaches. On a Friday or Saturday after reviewing my diet plan for the week, I would walk to the Whole Foods Market® nearby to purchase the meats and poultry that required baking. On a Sunday after breakfast, I would arrange the purchased items in baking dishes and place them in a cold oven. Then armed with a shopping list for the non-meat, non-poultry items for the week and my purse, I would turn on the oven, race for the door, and head to Whole Foods. When I returned from shopping, I would leave my purchases outside the door and race again to shut off the oven. I would transfer the cooked food to glass freezer-storage containers, avoiding plastic in any form, as Dr. Rea had recommended. During the week I heated the frozen food on the stove top, which I could tolerate. This is the way I cooked while I was in treatment at the clinic. There were times, of course, when I was too sick from testing or detoxing to shop or cook, but generally this was the approach I used.

The third consideration was washing clothes. Since I couldn't be near washers and dryers when they were operating, I needed to avoid running into other people in the laundry room using either the washers or dryers. I started getting up before five in the morning to do my wash, but I knew I did not want to do that indefinitely. One day another patient, Kathy Treat, and I were sitting in my apartment and the subject of the laundry room came up. We had both noticed how difficult it was to have time in the laundry room because there was no set schedule. We came up with a plan, which we laid out on notebook paper in the form of a grid by day of the week and two-hour time slot. I offered to present our plan to Earl, which I did that evening. He liked the idea and put it into effect.

The final consideration was testing and treatment at the clinic. For an EMF-sensitive person there are a number of hurdles to cross at the clinic. First, for some an overhead light can be a source of discomfort, even the full-spectrum lights in the clinic, which are thought to be better in general for everyone but in particular for EI patients. To accommodate EMF-sensitive patients, in testing room B the lights on one side of the room are kept turned off. I set up camp on that side of the room whenever I tested. Second, taking a sauna in the sauna treatment area, which has a treadmill, air cleaners, and three saunas operating, requires special precautions. At the time of my first visit to the clinic, there was another EMF-sensitive patient in treatment. The clinic manager set aside the hours between 8:30 a.m. and 10:00 a.m. Monday through Friday for us to sauna with all of the electrical equipment turned off. Jayne or the other sauna therapy staff would turn off the saunas and unplug all of the equipment. Then they would call us to come in. We were able to sauna in a turned-off ceramic sauna that retained heat at about 140 degrees during our sessions. Third, there are overhead lights and air cleaners in the consulting rooms. I asked for the lights and the air cleaner to be turned off whenever I had a consultation with Dr. Rea. Fourth, transportation to and from the clinic was provided at the time by Earl and his son. I managed the trips by sitting in the back of their cars on the right side. Somehow the EMF from the computer behind the dashboard did not bother me there.

Holistic Psychotherapy

Now that I had figured out a way to manage my life with EMF sensitivity, I began to think about how I was handling all these developments emotionally. Fortunately, in the last conversation I had had with my sister, Arleen, who was completing her Ph.D. program in psychology, she urged me to talk to the psychotherapist who counsels Dr. Rea's patients. Quite frankly, I couldn't see the point of more talk therapy. With an M.A. in counseling and years as a devotee of Murray Bowen's family systems therapy, I thought I knew everything about my psyche and significant relationships that I needed to know. Luckily, I heeded my sister's advice and made an appointment.

The person I encountered was unlike any other psychotherapist I had ever met. If I were to choose one word to describe the approach Dr. Carol Cole used, it would be "holistic" in the best sense of that word. Exploratory conversation covered a broad range of body-mind-spirit issues in addition to the usual review of biographical information and thinking and feeling states. This approach, coupled with her sensitivity to her patients' emotions, enables her to provide counseling with a unique perspective. After determining that I was a writer, she asked me to write about a trauma that I had experienced as a seven-year-old (sexual molestation by a stranger who lured me away from where I was playing in our neighborhood). I was not happy with this assignment. First of all, I had explored this incident with other therapists, and I thought I had dealt with it. Second, writing was something I did for a living. *How could it be therapeutic for me?* I asked for guidelines. She said she'd leave that to me.

"After all," she said, "you're a writer. You decide."

Over the next few days, I thought about the approach I would take. Having discussed this incident with other therapists, I didn't see any merit in just retelling the story. I opted, instead, to tell the story as my seven-year-old self. I adopted the approach of printing in large block letters, writing in short sentences, and using a simple vocabulary. The night before my next appointment, I sat at the table in the apartment with a blank sheet of paper and a pencil before me. I picked up the pencil and began printing *my name is* ....When I reached the end of the story, I burst into tears. I sobbed for what seemed like forever. When I finally stopped crying, I realized that I had had a cathartic release unlike anything I had ever experienced. The words chosen by my seven-year-old self had had a powerful effect. I had relived the experience and understood the bewilderment and fear I had felt as a child.

Psychotherapy that had targeted my psyche but ignored my spirit or soul, where the real hurt resided, had only touched the surface of the sorrow I had carried since childhood. That insult to my soul began healing when Dr. Cole suggested I write about it, and I called upon my seven-year-old self to tell her story. In an interview published in the *New York Times,* November 3, 1957, Isak Dinesen (the Danish storyteller movingly portrayed by Meryl Streep in *Out of Africa)*, in answer to a question raised by interviewer Bent Mohn, replied in part: "One of my friends said about me that I think all sorrows can be borne if you put them into a story or tell a story about them...." I would amend that to "all sorrows *can begin to be healed* when you tell a story about them, for storytelling touches the soul."

7 ARASINI FOUNDATION

Late November 2002

Roger arrived for another visit the weekend before week five. He was working at the apartment when the call came from the Arasini Foundation one morning that I could be seen that afternoon. He picked me up at the clinic, and we drove to the appointment together. Having no knowledge of energy medicine, neither one of us knew what to expect. We knew, however, that I needed help with the EMF sensitivity if we were to return to our normal life together. Now, in addition to stripping and bathing the moment he reached the apartment in Dallas, Roger could not use the telephone or watch television, and he had to sit in the dark when I was in the apartment. As for me, at this point, after over two weeks of feeling electricity coursing through my body, I was desperate for someone or something to turn it off.

We followed directions to the address we had been given. Roger drove, and I sat in the back seat of our car on the right side. When we reached our destination, we got out of the car and walked up to the door. I rang the bell. The door was opened by an attractive woman with short dark hair, very professionally dressed. She could have passed for one of my colleagues in public health consulting. We introduced ourselves.

"I'm not Deborah. We're still with a client. Make yourselves comfortable here, and we'll be out to get you."

Roger and I seated ourselves. We knew we couldn't talk much because our voices would be heard in the treatment room. We sat in silence. I thought about the person we had just met. I had been surprised by her appearance. I hadn't been expecting someone who looked professional. What had I been expecting? My sister had told me about receiving *Reiki* energy treatments from a massage therapist. Had I been expecting someone dressed in scrubs?

Deborah Singleton

My reverie was interrupted by an invitation for us to come into the treatment room. Seated on the opposite side of a treatment table that took up most of the space in the room was a woman with coiffed blonde hair, wearing a dress with a matching jacket and pumps. She introduced herself as Deborah Singleton and invited us to be seated. The woman we had met earlier was there along with another. Deborah introduced them as members of her healing team. They sat quietly and smiled at us.

Deborah began. "Well, Jennie, why don't you tell us why you were referred here?"

I did my best to recount the incident at the apartment. Deborah listened intently. When I was finished speaking, she asked questions about my symptoms, much as a physician would in taking a history. Throughout the discussion she looked at me, but it felt as if she were looking through me.

Addressing both of us, she said: "What do you know about energy work?" We admitted we knew nothing about it.

"Energy moves through pathways in the body called 'meridians.' Sometimes these pathways can become blocked, resulting in illness. In addition, as with electromagnetic fields generated by appliances, wires, and so on, the body's energy emanates as fields that extend out from the body. If a breach or imbalance occurs in these fields, energy from outside sources can penetrate to the physical body, causing the reactions Jennie is experiencing."

It sounded straightforward. "What do you do to change this breach in my energy fields?"

The healers would make an assessment, Deborah explained, and give me an energy balancing treatment. I was asked to sign a document granting permission for the Arasini healers to touch my body. I did so. Roger left the room and the treatment began.

As I lay on the table I felt the hands of three healers working on my head, stomach, and feet. There was a sensation of heat coming from their hands, which was pleasant and had a relaxing effect. About 15 minutes into the treatment I distinctly felt the electric prickliness I had been experiencing stop, and relief flooded my body. I didn't know how the healers were doing what they were doing, but at that point I didn't care. When the session ended, Deborah gave me oral and written instructions for grounding myself and using an energy reversal technique to balance my energy fields whenever I experienced an EMF reaction.

"Remember that energy follows thought and breath. You will use both in the visualization we've just given you. In the meantime, practice avoidance as much as possible."

"You mean in regard to things that emit electromagnetic fields?"

"Yes. The energy balancing will hold for a period of time. Then you will experience a return to dysfunctional energy patterns. With each balancing session, your patterns will become stronger and the effects of balancing will last longer. The energy balancing will work together with the chemical detoxifying you are experiencing through the treatment program at the clinic. You will become well again."

"How many treatments will I need?"

"There is no way to predict, Jennie."

"Will it be a matter of weeks or months?"

"Months, maybe longer."

As Roger and I drove back to the apartment, we discussed my assessment.

"Can we afford to have me stay in Dallas several months?"

"We'll work it out," Roger said.

"Are you comfortable with my continuing with energy treatment?"

"Yes," he said. "Very impressive presentation. I am confident you are in good hands."

I was amazed. Roger is a physician and epidemiologist with expertise in clinical trials, yet he was willing to support energy treatment, based on Deborah's presentation. The positive reaction I had had on the treatment table confirmed his opinion. In retrospect, I should not have been surprised. My husband is an open-minded, intuitive man whose gut feelings about people have often been validated. My feelings were equally positive. There was an air of authority around Deborah Singleton that felt somehow "right" to me. I, too, thought that I was in good hands, but had someone asked me why I thought so at that moment, I could not have said why. I was about to embark on a great journey, to be purged and forged through the divine fire of awakening, and I was right where I needed to be, having been brought face to face with the person who was to guide me through the beginnings of my awakening.

I discussed the energy treatment in my next counseling session with Dr. Cole. It was then I learned that many healers believe the body stores emotions from traumatic events as energy blocks in the body's energy pathways. Releasing these blocks and restoring energetic balance would allow the body and psyche to heal. I had had massage and acupuncture treatments several years earlier from a healer who was a student at the Traditional Acupuncture Institute in Columbia, Maryland. I was, therefore, somewhat familiar with the concept of energy moving through meridians and the need to release energy blocks. I was also vaguely familiar with the concept of stored emotions in the body, for I had experienced emotional pain when my so-called grief points were treated during an acupuncture session in Maryland. My background as a public health writer and editor, however, despite years of reading in areas ranging from substance abuse and mental illness to maternal and child health and cardiovascular disease, had not prepared me at all for the world in which I found myself, where a ringing telephone could cause pain in my chest. With no other remedies in sight, I decided to be open to whatever the healers in Dallas suggested to me.

Meditation

After my next energy balancing treatment, in response to my asking what I could do to help myself, Deborah suggested I meditate. *Meditate? I have no experience with meditation,* I thought. *I've prayed, of course, but meditate?*

"Is there something I need to think about or recite to get started?" I asked.

"Not really. Call the light to you and sit quietly. Let your mind be still and see what comes to you."

Let my mind be still? For years I had carried paperback books with me to read whenever I had to wait anywhere just so I could avoid the anxiety I felt when sitting still with nothing to do. *Okay. If this is what I need to do to heal, I'll try it. Anything to stop feeling electricity in my body.*

The next day I began what became a daily practice, meditation every morning and evening. Naively, I meditated to *achieve* "stillness," a point at which thoughts in my mind would be stilled. I concentrated on breathing in and out slowly and listening to the sounds of inhalation and exhalation. It was a humbling experience for me. I could not keep my mind "still," or empty, for more than a few seconds. The mind chatter was incessant. Once again, I sought advice from Deborah.

"Recognize with love the thoughts that intrude and just allow them to be. Accept them as a part of who you are, Jennie. Then take a deep breath, and begin again."

I did as instructed, but it was unbelievably frustrating. I finally just set a limit on the time I would attempt to be still. Then I sent love and light to all souls everywhere, with an offer of healing should they choose to accept, as Deborah had counseled me to do, praying for healing for us all. In time, the stillness would come. First, however, I had to understand that stillness isn't achieved as a result of willful effort. It is a gift that comes through intention and openness to the experience. When you are ready for stillness, it comes to you.

Being Present

Sometime during the third week of treatment at Arasini, Deborah recommended I read *The Power of Now* by Eckhart Tolle and introduced a new practice to me, that of "being present."

"Strive to be mindful of what you are experiencing in any moment. You can start by monitoring your thoughts for negativity. Then, whenever you observe a negative thought or feeling, surround it with white light, take a deep breath, and as you exhale, visualize it moving through you to your feet. Ask Mother Earth if she will accept it from you and with permission send it into the earth."

It was through this exercise, performed many times a day, that I began learning to "be present" and to monitor my thoughts to keep the energies around me positive. As the weeks passed, I kept to the following routine: early morning meditation; sauna therapy and skin testing sessions at the clinic; rotational use of antigens, incorporating new antigens as testing revealed new sensitivities; twice weekly intravenous infusions of vitamins, amino acids, and supplements; weekly consultations with Dr. Rea, during which we reviewed my progress and planned the next week's program; once a week appointments with the psychotherapist, Dr. Cole; twice a week energy balancing treatments at the Arasini Foundation; and continuous monitoring of my thoughts for negativity. At the end of each energy balancing treatment, I received additional balancing exercises to do on my own, and I added them to my daily practice. I learned to identify acupressure points and was taught to work on them to keep my energy pathways open. I was given visualization exercises and used them daily. I ended each day with meditation.

8 EDUCATION

December 2002

I began buying books to educate myself about environmental illness and energy medicine (see lists at back of book). Reading was a luxury I could indulge only between periods of detoxification. In the EI world, many people cannot read because of sensitivity to print. Some must "outgas" books for a certain length of time before handling them. Others can read only through a reading box. For me, sensitivity to print would come and go with the level of detoxification I was experiencing. As anyone who has been through a concentrated sauna detoxification program knows, toxins can leave the body in periodic bursts. Dr. Rea compares this process of shedding toxins to "peeling an onion." I always knew I was beginning to shed another layer because I could not touch a newspaper or a book. The smell of the print on the pages would nauseate me and irritate my small airways, causing pain in my chest. Given my profession, not being able to read from time to time was an agonizing deprivation, as it was to Roger. If his visits coincided with these periods, he could not read when we were together, and that truly was a hardship for him. Nevertheless, he strove to keep books and newspapers away from me.

When I was able to read, I read *Detoxify or Die* and *The EI Syndrome Revised* by Sherry A. Rogers, M.D., *Less-Toxic Alternatives* by Carolyn Gorman with Marie Hyde, and *Sauna Detoxification Therapy: A Guide for the Chemically Sensitive* by Marilyn McVicker. I learned that mold can grow unseen inside walls and ceilings and exposure to certain kinds of mold spores can make whole families ill. In fact, I was beginning to meet individuals and families at the clinic who had been sickened by mold. As I read about the toxic chemicals used in manufacturing building materials, cars, furnishings, plastics, clothing, personal care products (especially makeup), detergents and other cleaning agents, pesticides, and herbicides, I began to realize that we are exposed to toxins from an early age on, breathing them in, absorbing them through the skin, or ingesting them through the food we eat or the water we drink. Although I did not remember at the time, I now recall that as a young child I was exposed to the pesticides my community sprayed to kill mosquitoes during the summer months. I can remember playing outside, seeing the spraying trucks go by, and smelling the odor that lingered in the air after they had passed by. I can also recall periodically smelling the chlorine in our water and not wanting to drink it. I now recognize that I was exposed to the outgassing of new building materials as a teenager. I not only helped lay down a wood parquet floor with adhesives that I now suspect to have contained toxic chemicals, but also as soon as the flooring was set in the new room that was to be my bedroom, I moved into the room in the new addition to our house. Within three years of that move, at age 19, I was diagnosed with colitis and lactose intolerance. When I married and left my parents' home, my former husband and I were the first occupants of an apartment in a new apartment complex, where we were exposed to outgassing formaldehyde and phenols from the new construction materials as well as from all of our new furnishings. I began to suffer from vaginal yeast infections, which plagued me throughout my adult life. After a one-month trial on birth control pills, I developed migraine headaches (sometimes with and sometimes without aura), which then recurred three times a month, synchronous with the hormonal fluctuations of my menstrual cycle. We purchased and moved into a newly-renovated house. I had great difficulty conceiving and suffered a traumatic miscarriage before carrying my son to full term. Other health problems followed, including allergies to prescription medications. In my late thirties, after moving into a two-year-old house, I was diagnosed with reactive hypoglycemia and fibromyalgia within three years of that move. A pattern of exposure to outgassing chemicals followed by further health problems had emerged. Some might argue that anyone who looks hard enough can find a pattern in a series of unrelated events. What if, however, a common link existed? Mainstream medical researchers had been looking at toxic substances in makeup and other personal care products as possible triggers for the development of fibromyalgia. Roger and I had attended a presentation at Tulane by a doctoral student working with a seasoned researcher who was looking into just such a correlation. Everything I was reading in the books on environmental illness and learning at the EHC-D led me to drop whatever vestiges of doubt remained about the link between toxic exposure and my chronic illnesses. As I detoxed, I gave more thought to the possibility of discontinuing my medications for fibromyalgia, but I was not yet ready to take that step.

In addition to reading about environmental illness, at Deborah's suggestion I began reading Barbara Ann Brennan's *Hands of Light: A Guide to Healing Through the Human Energy Field* and Donna Eden's *Energy Medicine*. The information in both books helped me begin to understand how practitioners of energy medicine view the physical body and its energy system. Energy flows through pathways in the physical body called meridians, as Deborah had explained to Roger and me, as well as around the physical body in energetic layers called "energy fields" or "energy bodies." These energy fields generally reflect the emotional, cognitive, and spiritual aspects of an individual, and some of the fields are named after these aspects. The "emotional field" or "body," for instance, reflects the feelings one has, while the "mental field" or "body" reflects thoughts, belief systems, and the process of thinking itself. While the emotional and mental energy fields are generally identified by the same names by most healers, the several other fields are identified by various names, depending on the school of healing. Nevertheless, most healers agree that blockages at any point in the energy system create imbalances in the physical body or the energy fields and can lead to illness or less than optimal functioning of body systems. At this point, I did not understand fully how healers balance energy. Since I was benefiting so much from the treatments at the Arasini Foundation, I decided not to worry about what the healers were doing. For me, the effects of energy treatment could be dramatic at times. If, for instance, I had had acute reactions to allergens during testing, an energy balancing treatment would alleviate the symptoms I was experiencing.

Additional Changes in Perception

At the end of one of my energy balancing treatments, I confided to Deborah that I had experienced phenomena I could not explain. I had begun "seeing" colors when my eyes were closed— blues, greens, purples, reds, oranges, and golds of the richest hues I had ever encountered, so dazzling that I found it hard to describe them adequately. The colors had been coming, unbidden, into my consciousness, sometimes while meditating, often when receiving an energy treatment, and at other times when resting my eyes after reading.

"Deborah, do you know what I am seeing?"

"You are seeing the various frequencies of light."

"How am I doing this?"

"Your sixth chakra is beginning to open."

Ah, I thought, *some clarity.* The colors I had been seeing sometimes resembled a huge eye opening and closing within my forehead, the seat of the sixth chakra, or "third eye." I confided further that something in my hearing had changed. I had noticed when I was living in New Orleans that I was hearing what sounded like a high-pitched frequency continuously.

"Do I have tinnitus?"

"You may, or you may be hearing the energies around you."

The latter made sense to me, for I couldn't describe what I was hearing as ringing at all. Over time I would learn that I was, in fact, hearing the energies around me, for each time the vibration of my energy fields changed, the sound would become much louder. After my energy fields had, once again, stabilized, the sound would decrease. In the beginning, hearing energy was disconcerting to me. Eventually, I came to regard the sound as just a part of who I am, and I became comfortable with it. At that point in time, however, I was not really grasping what was happening to me. I knew that I was changing. I certainly didn't know where these changes would lead me or the impact they would have on me and on my relationships with other people. I continued to discuss these changes with Deborah and Dr. Cole. I did not talk to anyone else. If I couldn't explain the changes to myself, how could I explain them to someone else?

In mid-December, Roger and I discussed our options about where we could live following my treatment at the clinic and the Arasini Foundation. Dr. Rea recommended strongly that I not return to Louisiana because of the widespread use of pesticides there. In reviewing the toxin and pollution monitoring maps at the clinic, we observed that the clearest areas in the country were in Montana, northern Arizona, and northern New Mexico (except for the Los Alamos area). Dr. Rea concurred that the high desert areas of New Mexico would be a good place for us to try. Since Santa Fe was one of Roger's favorite U.S. cities, he asked me if I would consider a move there. Having never been there but trusting my husband's esthetic judgment of places, I said I would. He began to talk to people in the area: a Santa Fe architect who built environmentally safe houses, a realtor with lots for sale, and a chemically sensitive woman who was advertising guest rooms for rent but who was also considering selling and moving out of state. We made plans to drive to Santa Fe, but first we had to determine if I could cope with the electromagnetic fields to which I'd be exposed during the trip. We did a test drive in Texas, stopping every so often so I could use the grounding techniques I had learned. The test was not successful. We learned about a grounding wire that could be attached to the bottom of the car, with one end touching the driving surface and the other wired into the passenger section and attached to the wrist through a copper bracelet. We did another test run. It was a disaster. The grounding wire had the opposite effect on me, and I was electrified in a most painful way. We cancelled our trip.

We celebrated Christmas in the apartment in Dallas. Visits from Colin and my brother, Bill, his wife, Cheryl, and their family made it a happy occasion. Before the visits, we had to ask that everyone de-scent himself or herself. Everyone in the EI world knows how difficult it is to explain to people in the normal world just how devastating scent can be, whether the source is cologne, hairspray, fabric softener, laundry detergent, air fresheners, or scented candles. Scents are created from orris root or from other substances to which EI patients are highly reactive. Some of the saddest stories I've heard from other patients concerned their families' unwillingness to acknowledge environmental illness and cooperate by de-scenting themselves. I consider myself blessed that my family and friends understood and continued to de-scent themselves in order to visit me while I was in treatment and afterwards.

Avoidance

The isolation that one encounters in the EI world is one of the most devastating aspects of the experience. Only those who enter this world can truly appreciate the desperation of its inhabitants. In order to survive, they must practice avoidance. For some, that can mean living a life that is essentially homebound, unable to work or go to school, needing to depend on other people for life's essentials. For others, it can mean not being able to visit with friends and relatives who may be unwilling to de-scent themselves and make the environment in their houses tolerable. Many EI people cannot do the things that most of us take for granted, or they need to take special precautions in order to do them. Going to the supermarket, attending school, buying clothing, finding a safe place to live, all become challenges to be overcome because of the need to avoid scents, outgassing formaldehyde, or other toxins. When I was advised to wear shoes with leather soles to make it easier to keep myself grounded energetically, Roger drove me to a shoe store in Dallas. Knowing I couldn't enter the store because of the outgassing of all of the leather goods, he went inside alone and patiently explained to the clerks why I couldn't come in. As I sat outside the front door feeling unbelievably conspicuous, a clerk brought shoes to me to try on. As we drove away with the newly purchased shoes that would have to be outgassed in the sun before I could wear them, Roger confided to me that he had the distinct impression the clerks were highly suspicious of us.

"Perhaps they thought we were trying to pull a fast one," he said. I was mortified at the thought.

Avoidance is a two-edged sword. While it is absolutely necessary initially to ensure healing, for me, as well as for others I met in Dallas, it brought with it a chronic fear of exposure, which in turn became another obstacle to healing. Working through this fear was one of my biggest challenges. It was not until I recognized it and learned how to deal with it that I was able to believe I was well and return to the world I thought I had left forever.

9 EXPANDING CONSCIOUSNESS

January 2003 through February 2003

The longer I continued in Dr. Rea's treatment program, the more flexible my muscles felt. An interesting phenomenon had developed during provocative skin testing. Some of the substances I tested triggered muscle pain, which was then "turned off" when the right antigen endpoint was determined. I was beginning to see a relationship between my sensitivities and the pain that I associated with fibromyalgia. In addition, during saunas, I had the sensation that the muscle pain was melting away in the heat.

Progress, of course, always has its price. As the level of detoxification deepened, I experienced more acute symptoms during or after the saunas. Many times I became so nauseated I thought I would vomit. Other times I would have tremors or experience difficulty breathing. Sometimes these symptoms would be accompanied by emotional catharsis, also referred to as "clearing" or "releasing" by healers. I remember one catharsis, in particular, that was notable for the clarity of a memory that came forward spontaneously. I was sitting in one of the ceramic saunas alone, and I was perspiring profusely. I started to feel pain in my lower back. Suddenly, as if I were experiencing regression therapy, I felt myself back in my mother's womb. I was a first-born child, and it was a difficult birth. Forceps were being used to ease my passage into the world, and the forceps slipped, tearing the right side of my face. I felt my mother's pain when she saw the injury to my face, and I started sobbing. Jayne came running into the sauna. "Jennie, what's happening?"

"I'm not really sure. I had a painful memory."

"Don't worry. Crying in the sauna is not unusual." She handed me a towel. "Do you need to come out?"

"No. I can manage." Jayne left but kept an eye on me.

It was not until later in the day that I had time to think about what had happened. Having read about psychoanalytic regression therapy, I was able to put a name to the experience; however, I did not remember reading that these experiences could take place spontaneously. Generally, people undergoing regression therapy are hypnotized and guided back through younger and younger ages to the memory of their birth by their therapist. Because I had been by myself when the memory came forward, I had to look for another explanation. I had spoken to Deborah about memories that were coming forward and images that would suddenly appear in my mind during energy treatments.

"Think of memories and thoughts as energies," she said. "As we call your energies into balance, the integration that takes place during and after a balancing can trigger memories, sometimes in the form of thoughts and sometimes in images. And integration can take place over days, weeks, or months. It depends on what is being integrated and your personal process."

I had had energy balancing the day before. Could it be that the balancing was working in concert with the sauna detoxification to help me heal on many levels? I was willing to entertain the thought that I had just benefited from the interaction of these therapies.

The Body's Intelligence

I told Deborah about the incident in the sauna. "Why don't you try speaking to your pain the next time you experience it?"

Speak to my pain? Okaaay, I thought. *You promised to be open to everything, right?* I said to myself. *So go ahead.* There was no one more surprised than I when my pain spoke back to me. It was not "speaking" in the usual sense of the word. I was not "hearing voices." What came into my consciousness was information about the pain through images, memories, feelings, impressions, and, yes, words. But the voice I heard was my own, coming from an intelligence I had not yet identified. I suppose under other circumstances I might have been concerned about my mental stability. Because I had the ear of a strong mentor, whose every suggestion was leading me to explore my expanding consciousness, as well as the counseling of a sensitive psychotherapist, I never doubted the grace with which I was being visited.

As I worked with the healers at the Arasini Foundation and Dr. Cole, emotional issues that had been buried for a long time in my body's energies surfaced for release. Although I did not understand this at the time, my emotional field or "body" was beginning to clear itself, helped by the energy medicine, the psychotherapeutic process, and my expanding consciousness. As my emotional body cleared, I began feeling better and better in my physical body. Clearing dysfunctional energies through catharsis was, and still is, a very painful process for me, but it has been crucial to my healing. Moreover, it helped me to understand what I had been asked to do by nearly everyone who guided me, that is, to listen to my body. Listening to one's body was a foreign concept to me, as I think it is for most people. We live so much in our minds that we tend to shut ourselves off from our bodies and the possibility of organic intelligence. When I was first asked to listen to my body in Dallas, I remembered attending a conference at Georgetown University and observing a presentation by Dr. Candace Pert, who spoke of a neuronal language that could communicate stress to the body right down to the cellular level. It was an easy next step to think of those neuronal language pathways as bi-directional and to accept the possibility that my cells and organs might be able to communicate to me on several levels of consciousness. Years later, as I was preparing this book for publication, I would be guided to a book written by Dr. Pert, *Molecules of Emotion*, published a few years after her appearance at the Georgetown conference. In this book, she described in scientific terms the consciousness of what she termed the "bodymind," explaining the function of messenger molecules that carried information from and to every cell in the body, proposing that thoughts and emotions affect the health of the physical body through the linkage of emotional messenger molecules with cells.

How did I learn to listen to my body? I began simply by not ignoring what I was feeling, not very easy for someone who had worked on deadline-driven projects through fevers and migraines. Now, if I felt tired, I rested. If I felt pain, I did not ignore it. I asked simple questions of my body's intelligence and waited for answers to surface in any form, whether by memory, image, feeling, or words and phrases. It was trial and error, but the more I attempted to access information in this way, the easier it became to do so. The progression was simple. The more I trusted my body's intelligence, the more successful I was in accessing it and confirming its wisdom. Then, in what turned out to be a major test of trust, a feeling came to me that I needed to stop taking guaifenesin for fibromyalgia. I stopped it "cold turkey" without consequences.

The Wider Realm of the Soul

Communication with the body's intelligence led me to sense the wider realm of the soul. I was beginning to feel more and more connected to the consciousness of who we are. And it seemed so normal to me, so familiar, in a way I could not articulate. I sensed an energetic presence around me, a presence that was loving, non-judgmental, and protective, and I wanted to understand what I was sensing. I began communicating with this presence. Images, memories, single words, or phrases would come into my consciousness whenever I needed assurance or guidance. What I felt most of all from this presence was unconditional love. I was reminded of how I had felt the moment my son was placed in my arms as I lay in a recovery area after giving birth. Love had come pouring into me and through me to him in a way I had not known was possible. One day, filled with this love, I asked if the presence had a name. I was startled when the words "Blessed Mother" flashed through my mind. Although I had begun praying to Jesus and Mary again in New Orleans, I had not been a practicing Catholic for years, and "Blessed Mother" is the name by which the mother of Jesus is usually known to Catholics. Moreover, for years I had believed that anyone could have a personal relationship with God through any belief system. To me, what was in a person's heart was what mattered most. At that moment in Dallas, I could speculate only that as my consciousness expanded I was becoming more aware of my soul's energies and able to receive divine communication as mystics had done before me. Because this communication had come to me through a familiar route, my childhood beliefs, I was completely open to it. I welcomed it, gradually realizing that there was no "on" or "off" to it. It was just a part of who I was, and I began living in two worlds simultaneously, the secular and the spiritual, communicating with the Blessed Mother as I communicated with the people around me. Of course, to make sure I remained grounded as I continued to open, I spoke to both Deborah and Dr. Cole, both of whom encouraged me to develop this spiritual relationship.

10 SENSITIVITY TO ENERGIES

March 2003

Even as my consciousness was expanding, empirical evidence was reinforcing and confirming what I was learning about energy from the healers in Dallas. As a result of becoming sensitive to electromagnetic fields and experiencing energy movement during both energy treatments and my own practice of energy balancing, I quickly came to accept the existence of energy flows and energy fields, or "bodies." It is one thing to read what other people have written or to hear what they have to say about energy movement through and around the body; it is another thing entirely to experience energy movement and to feel energy that emanates from other people. How does energy feel? That depends on the source of the energy as well as on the moment. For example, to imagine how free-flowing energy feels within the physical body, picture a garden hose with the nozzle set to a fine spray. Then imagine the feeling of water moving gently through the nozzle onto your hand like a mist rather than a flow. If you've ever visited the outdoor patio of a restaurant in southern Arizona during the really hot months and felt the spray from the outdoor misters, you will know how the mist feels against the skin. Think of how that would feel if it were to flow through your body. That is the way free-flowing energy feels in the body once you have become sensitive to it. Sometimes it feels warm, but other times it feels very cool. Sometimes it flows continuously, but other times it pulses. When I first practiced energy balancing exercises, I felt only faint movement, and generally just for the duration of the exercises. The more I practiced, however, the more conscious I became of energy movement within my physical body, even when I was not deliberately monitoring the flows.

When energy flows are blocked, however, the blocked energy

can sometimes manifest itself as pain of varying intensity. For example, like most people, I tend to hold tension in my neck, which can be painful. To ease the tension, Elizabeth Ellison, a certified massage therapist then working at A Healing Place, taught me to massage certain acupressure points under my arms and to trace the spaces between my ribs, finishing by massaging the bottom of the rib cage on both sides of the body in an upward motion. That approach never fails to ease the tension in my neck. The massage techniques energize acupressure points along meridians in the torso, shoulders, and neck, freeing energy blocks and allowing the neck muscles to relax. Because of my sensitivity to energy movement, after using this technique, I not only feel my neck relax but I also feel energy flow through my neck muscles. Finally, energy flows can be uncomfortable, not only during the releasing of an energy block but also during the clearing of an EMF reaction. Whenever I used the energy reversal technique Deborah taught me to dissipate an EMF reaction, the feeling of energy in the body was intense, prickly, and mildly painful.

Other People's Energies

Feeling another person's energies can sometimes be uncomfortable as well, something I experienced for the first time one day in Dallas. I heard a knock at the apartment door.

"Hello, Maggie." I had met Maggie earlier in the day at the clinic.

"Do you have time to talk to me?"

Since Roger was resting and I didn't want to disturb him, I said I would join her outside. I put on a windbreaker, stepped outside, and closed the door.

"They told me at the clinic today that I have EMF sensitivity."

"What bothers you?"

"Everything. Telephones, television, cell phones, the electricity in the apartment. Someone at the clinic said you have

EMF and you are doing better. What are you doing to feel better?"

"I'm receiving energy balancing from the healers at the Arasini Foundation and continuing treatment at Dr. Rea's clinic."

"Dr. Rea referred me to Arasini, but I have to wait for an opening in the schedule there. I'm going crazy. How do you stand it?" She burst into tears.

I touched her arm lightly. "Let me show you an exercise I learned at Arasini. It is a clearing exercise."

She dried her tears. "Okay."

"Stand on the earth next to the sidewalk and face me. Picture a column of light above your head. As you inhale, draw the light down and through your body to your feet. Ask Mother Earth to accept the light from you. With permission, send that light deep into the earth, asking for grounding energies in return. See green light, the color of grass coming up from the earth into your feet and then through your body and out the top of your head. See yourself as a fountain spouting green water."

At that moment, she took a step toward me, and I felt a shock to my chest that made me step back. She stepped toward me again, and shocked again, I stepped back.

"Please stop," I said. Not knowing how to explain what I was feeling, I said: "You need to stay in one spot for the exercise to work." She stood still.

"Now see a circle of energy moving around your body clockwise. Stop it, and send it in reverse." We held the visualization for about two minutes.

"Now stop the reverse circular movement and send the movement clockwise again. Breathe deeply."

I watched as the tension in her face loosened. "Better?"

"Yes. Thank you so much."

I later related this incident to Deborah, who explained to me that I had felt a disturbance in the woman's energy fields. *Well,* I thought to myself, *I suppose it is no surprise that I can feel someone else's energies now that I've become sensitive to my own.*

Healing and Forgiveness

As I worked with the healers at the Arasini Foundation, met with Dr. Cole, and continued reading about energy fields, I came to recognize the relationship between illness in the body and unresolved issues with the people in our lives through their effects on our energy systems. Since I had been learning that imbalanced energy leads to illness, I considered what effects those unresolved issues might have on the people in my life as well as on me. I resolved to do whatever I could to heal any misunderstandings I had been a part of, taking full responsibility for my part and asking for forgiveness. I began writing letters, each of which carried the intention of bringing healing to the other person as well as to me. The response to my letters brought me my heart's desire, for I regained the love of two people I had admired all my life but from whom I had been cut off as a result of misunderstanding. From the re-establishment of those relationships came the re-establishment of others. Even today, I continue to heal relationships in my life through letters and phone calls. Not all of my overtures have met with success, but I continue to reach out, nevertheless.

Trip to Santa Fe

Later in the month, I noticed I was feeling stronger and was much less EMF-reactive during car trips. I began to think that I could make the trip to Santa Fe. Anticipating that we would have to judge the "safety" of the house we had been invited to see, that is, whether the house was sufficiently free of toxins so that I could live in it, I bought, read, and shared with Roger two books that were very helpful: *The Healthy House* by John Bower and *Prescriptions for A Healthy House* by Paula Baker-Laporte, Erica Elliott, and John Banta. Roger made arrangements for us to break the journey in Amarillo at La Casita del Sol, an inn with hardwood floors, run by innkeeper Bonnie Rodriguez, who keeps an organic garden and cleans with vinegar and baking soda. The inn did have some drawbacks for which we had to prepare: gas heat (I used an antigen), paintings and scented sheets (Bonnie removed these from the room we stayed in). We brought our own bed linens, an Austin air cleaner, food, antigens, and water in glass bottles. We had been advised to stop every hour for me to ground myself and use the EMF-reversal technique. We did so, and I marveled at my husband's patience.

It was not an easy trip for either one of us. Roger had to do all of the driving, while I sat in the back of the car away from the car's computer. Although I dutifully grounded myself, the EMF exposure caught up with me at night, and I found it impossible to sleep. When we arrived in Santa Fe, we followed directions to the home of the chemically sensitive woman to whom my husband had spoken months earlier. We found ourselves on top of one of the Sangre de Cristo Mountains southeast of downtown Santa Fe with views of Santa Fe and surrounding mountain ranges. We gingerly extracted ourselves from the car after our bumpy ride up the mountain road. The minute my feet hit the earth, the word "home" came into my consciousness. Although neither one of us said anything at the time, we confided to each other later that each of us had had the same thought, namely, that Providence had led us to this place. While Roger was looking around, I walked toward the front door, which was open. I knocked, walked in, and introduced myself to the owner, our hostess. Roger followed.

The house felt wonderfully safe. The flooring was of slate throughout. The walls had been covered with vegetable-based paint. The heating system was electric. The water coming into the house was artesian, and the owner gave us a copy of a full-spectrum water analysis showing water of very good quality. The only drawback I could see was the pine ceilings. After two days in the house with no reactions, I was willing to consider a longer trial period in the house. Although we did see a realtor and looked at property in another area, we decided to accept the owner's invitation to rent the main floor of the house with the idea of testing the house and negotiating to buy it. We returned from Santa Fe with hope that we could have a normal life again.

11 DARK NIGHT OF THE SOUL

April 2003 through July 2003

When we returned from our trip to Santa Fe, Roger and I met with Dr. Rea to discuss our move to the house on the mountain. We showed him the full-spectrum analysis of the water supply the owner had provided as well as photos of the interior and exterior of the house. While he, too, had reservations about the pine ceilings, he recommended that we live in the house without furniture or curtains for several months before deciding to buy it. We made plans to leave Dallas as soon as possible, thinking we might be able to go in mid-May.

Toward the end of April, however, Roger began to feel ill. In one of our early morning calls, after he had quickly described his symptoms to me, I suddenly remembered my son's experience with shingles. I knew the memory was not accidental. I urged Roger to see our dermatologist. My intuition was confirmed by our doctor's diagnosis. Despite treatment with antiviral drugs, Roger lay ill with shingles for nearly five weeks, losing 30 pounds in the process. I was bereft. Roger was in New Orleans, and I was in Dallas. There was no way for me to be with him to nurse him through this debilitating illness. I did the only things I could do: I sent him love from my heart every morning and evening, and I pleaded with him to accept help from my sister and friends who had offered to shop for him and bring him food. Roger doesn't cook, and I knew that eating nutritious food would help him recover. Of course, I wondered, as anyone would under the circumstances, why we were separated at a time when Roger needed my help. I was to have my answer shortly.

Transtemporal Perception

A week after Roger was diagnosed with shingles, on a Friday just after I had returned from the clinic, I started to feel pain in my lower spine. As the hours went by, the pain intensified. As I had been doing since realizing that I had opened to my soul, I grounded myself and meditated. I sat in a chair with my feet firmly on the floor. I concentrated on my feet. I felt excruciating pain, but I was focused. Questions formulated themselves, and answers came forward.

What is happening to me?

Clearing and releasing.

What am I clearing?

See.

Memories flooded my consciousness. I had read accounts of near-death experiences in which people said that the events of their entire lives had flashed before their eyes. Like them, I found myself in a tunnel of white light, remembering all the hurts and joys of my life. I was a seven-year-old again. I was playing outside with my sister and friends. A young man appeared out of nowhere.

"You look like a smart girl. Can you help me find my lost puppy?"

I looked up at the man. I wasn't looking at him through a seven-year-old's eyes. I was seeing him through an adult's eyes. He looked disheveled and gave the appearance of limited mental capacity.

"What does your dog look like?"

"He is really tiny with black curly hair."

"Oh, he sounds so cute. Yes, I'll help you."

"I knew you were smart enough to help me."

I swelled with pride as I walked away unknowingly with the man who would molest me. *What am I feeling? Am I feeling the emotions of my seven-year-old self as if I were there again?*

You are, Jennie.

How is that possible?

Transtemporal experience.

Transtemporal experience? Oh, no. I can't relive this experience. Take it away.

Your work and your trust in your process have called this forth for you to release.

Too painful. I can't do this.

Say to yourself, "I let it go."

I let it go?

Yes.

I let it go. I let it go. I let it go!

An incredible amount of information was streaming into my consciousness, and it was painful emotionally and physically. Just as it reached the point where I thought I could not tolerate more pain, I felt a rush of energy from the bottom of my spine up and out of my head. If I had seen blood, I would have thought my head had blown open. I started sobbing uncontrollably. When the sobbing subsided, I found myself lying on the mattress on the floor of the apartment exhausted. My head ached, and my nose was sore. I could hardly breathe through the congestion brought on by the weeping. *It's over now. I know it is. I can't take any more.*

Past Lives

The process started again. Only this time, the nature of the memories changed. I started to remember other times, other civilizations. It seemed as if a temporal veil had been torn away, and I was flying through time. I felt myself a character in a play with a continuously changing plot. Suddenly, I was far away. I was standing on top of a very high place and looking down at the movement of people on the ground. I was watching them carefully. *Who are they? Who am I?* Sorrow overwhelmed me. The scene changed. I saw a robed figure walking along a dirt road. No. I wasn't watching. I was that person. *Where am I?* The pain in my lower spine intensified. I felt a sudden rush up my spine into and out of my head. I sobbed.

Blessed Mother, are you here?

I'm right next to you. I felt her presence on my right side.

See me.

How?

You know how. Remember. I saw a figure of dazzling white light.

Am I seeing you?

You are.

Barbara Brennan in *Hands of Light* refers to this kind of "seeing" as "higher sensory perception." Others call it "inner vision."

I am developing inner vision?

You are remembering how to see.

Deborah had told me that if my vision were to open it was because I was remembering how to see. Now her words were being reinforced.

Help me, please. I can't do this anymore.

The light intensified. I saw another figure. *Jesus?*

A hand of light reached out to me. I touched it. I dissolved into pure energy. I moved through a door of light. I was standing before what looked like a throne of golden light. I was transfixed.

Welcome, Jennie. Will you keep your promises?

My promises?

Your soul tasks. You have a mission to complete.

Yes.

Do you do this freely?

I do.

I started to shiver. I was drenched in sweat and fully in my body again.

I did not go to the clinic on Monday morning. I was too weak to shower or dress myself. I lay on the mattress all day, experiencing cycles of agonizing pain and altered consciousness. On Tuesday, I managed to shower and dress in time to be driven to the Arasini Foundation for my two o'clock appointment.

A Healing Crisis

"You are having a healing crisis," Deborah explained.

"A healing crisis?"

"You've become well enough to open and release very old energies. This is not a bad thing."

"The pain is beyond description."

"How are you coping with it?"

I looked at Deborah intently. She was seated in the same chair in which she had been sitting the first time I met her. "I feel like a warrior locked in battle. I feel strong despite the incredible pain."

"Good. Remember that you asked for this to happen in this way."

"I did?"

"You did, Jennie. On some level of who you are you planned for this to happen in this lifetime when you were ready. Now let's see how we can help you."

The pain overwhelmed my ability to think or speak. I surrendered myself to the work. At the end of the session, I sat up on the side of the table.

"Walking the path you've chosen is not easy. It is very painful. That is why many people who start on this path, leave it. It becomes too difficult for them."

"I will not leave the path." *What am I saying? Am I crazy? Do I want to live in pain the rest of my life?* Aloud I said: "Will this last long?"

"I really can't predict. This is a major change for you. I can say this: over time it will get easier. I can't say how long it will take to get to that point."

Della Estrada in the August 1992 issue of *Arizona Light* defined a healing crisis as "a period of change which a person passes through in order to cleanse, regenerate and become more healthy." I experienced this healing crisis as a body-mind-soul detoxification, which mystics call the "dark night of the soul."

For me, it was as wondrous as it was terrifying, a sort of metaphysical face-off with all I had been, in the present lifetime as well as in other lifetimes and other civilizations, in expressions of both darkness and light. Despite the fact that this dark night was unlike anything I had experienced before, somehow I knew I had the mental and physical fortitude to endure it. And I was right where I needed to be, with mentors close by and the Blessed Mother and Jesus to guide me when the process seemed ready to engulf me.

It was the first of many acute healing crises that would take place over the next seven years, and it lasted four weeks. I was in too much pain to go to the clinic. I could not sit for long in a chair. Other than my twice-weekly visits for energy balancing, I stayed in the apartment. Earl and his son, as well as the friends I had made at the apartment, bought groceries for me. There were times I could not stand, cook, or eat. I lay on the mattress on the floor of the apartment in Dallas in excruciating pain, experiencing altered states of consciousness, having emotional catharses three times a day. I was faced with a choice that many people have faced. I could either let the pain get the best of me on every level, emotional, physical, mental, spiritual, or I could accept what I was guided to understand—that it was a necessary part of the healing process that would bring me to a new level of wellness and openness to the realm of the soul. I believed that this stage of spiritual growth would pass, and I considered myself blessed. Blessed by the grace I was receiving. Blessed by my growing ability to communicate with the realm of the soul. Where this would lead me, how this would affect my relationships with the people I loved, I had no idea. I knew only that this transformation had to go forward.

Toward the end of May Roger felt fit enough to drive from New Orleans to Dallas. After consultations with Dr. Rea and Deborah Singleton, we began preparations to move to Santa Fe. Both Dr. Rea and Deborah thought I would have a better chance of recovering from EMF sensitivity in a more rural setting away from the high-tension wires and cell phone towers that are ubiquitous in Dallas. It was a community undertaking. Since Roger and I were not well enough to do much packing, Anne Reach, another friend from the apartments, and Kathy Treat came by after clinic visits to do it for us. Earl helped in so many ways. He shopped for us, buying towels to replace the ones we had had in New Orleans. He bought packing materials and helped us box what we needed to ship, and then he took the boxes to UPS. The energy and kindness of the people who helped us were gifts for which we will always be grateful.

Our Santa Fe Home

We left Dallas on the last day of May, arriving at our new home on June 1. Following Dr. Rea's advice, we lived without curtains and with very little furniture so that I could test my reactivity to the house. We ordered a futon, pillows, and bed linens, all made of organic cotton, from Bright Futures, a shop in Albuquerque, New Mexico, that specializes in safer, environmentally friendly products for bedrooms. In order to buy a futon or mattress without flame retardant, which contains chemicals I needed to avoid, I had to present a prescription for a flame retardant-free mattress/futon. I called Dr. Rea for one, which was faxed to the owner of the shop.

Once again, Roger and I slept on the floor. We were both weak—Roger from his bout with shingles and I from detoxification. We had to become acclimated to living at 8,000 feet, and for the next three months we dealt with the usual symptoms— shortness of breath, headaches, and nosebleeds. My healing crisis continued, but the acute pain was controlled by medications Dr. Rea prescribed for me. Now that we were living together again and Roger was able to observe what I was experiencing, he raised the question of whether I should start taking guaifenesin again. I assured him that the pain of the spinal releases associated with the healing crisis was different from that of fibromyalgia. It tended to be localized near the spine, and it was generally relieved by an emotional catharsis, indicating to me that the pain was associated with another change in my energy system. As difficult as it was for me to endure this first healing crisis, it was just as difficult for Roger to observe. The emotional pain I experienced was beyond ordinary description, so my attempts at explaining this pain to him were hardly adequate.

"You tell me you're not sad," he said to me on a few occasions. "Then why are you weeping?"

"I'm clearing something through my energy fields. It is very painful emotionally and physically, but I'm not sad in the usual sense of the word. When the weeping ends, I feel better."

"Have you discussed this with Deborah Singleton?"

"I have."

"And Carol Cole?"

"Yes. They will confirm that this clearing is a part of my healing."

I was grateful that Roger accepted what I said. So much trans-temporal information about my pain, about the pain of others, as well as the pain of the earth, for which I had no explanation that would be seen as rational by someone who was not experiencing the same thing, was coming into my consciousness. I was an awakening soul, experiencing life-altering changes in perception, and I felt incapable of discussing these changes with the people I loved. I didn't realize at the time that this reluctance was part of the ego's struggle for survival, for the more I identified with my higher self or soul, the less I identified with my ego self. It, therefore, asserted itself through the fear that I would be somehow less acceptable to those I loved if I revealed the changes taking place in me. It would not be until September 2008, after reading a friend's copy of Eckhart Tolle's *A New Earth: Awakening to Your Life's Purpose*, that I could articulate the struggle of this period.

As the healing crisis ran its course, the frequency of emotional catharses changed from daily to weekly, but I encountered a new phenomenon, one I ascribe to the elevation at which we were living. The intense weeping during the catharses caused bleeding into the skin around my eyes. With periodic shiners the size of tennis balls on both eyes, I took to wearing sunglasses whenever I was around other people, which wasn't often. For the most part, we lived in isolation on the mountain.

It was much easier to avoid electromagnetic fields in our new home. All of the appliances were situated at one end of the house. There was no air conditioning and no need for it. Living in a climate with extremely low humidity and the nearly constant movement of air at high elevations kept the house comfortable even during the rare periods when the temperatures soared. The house was designed to be solar efficient, so that it would not get too hot in summer and could take advantage of heat from the sun in winter, requiring the use of only a few strategically placed electric baseboard units. We took advantage of our location, far away from traffic, opening windows and allowing the fresh mountain breezes to blow through the house. I had taken the precaution of testing at the EHC-D for sensitivity to the region's trees, grasses, and weeds and then taking the appropriate antigens. That paid off. I've never had a symptom related to any of the pollination periods around Santa Fe. We lived without television, radio, cell phones, and computer. I could talk on our land-line phone for up to fifteen minutes before I would feel pain in my hand and arm. The EMF reactions were no longer penetrating to my chest. At the end of every telephone conversation I would use the energy reversal exercise I had learned in Dallas to calm my energy fields.

12 LIFE IN SANTA FE

August 2003 through January 2004

At the end of August, Roger returned to New Orleans to complete one more semester at Tulane University before retiring. My first healing crisis had resolved, and I was driving again. The plan was that Roger would fly home once every three weeks for a weekend visit. In the meantime, I would be on my own. Trips into town for groceries provided contact with other people, as did weekly lessons in Tibetan. I still wasn't able to use a computer, but I was able to read again. I decided to explore a vision I had had in Dallas indicating a connection between Tibetans and Navajos, a conviction that is shared by others, in particular Peter Gold, author of *Navajo & Tibetan Sacred Wisdom: The Circle of the Spirit*. As someone interested in the structure of language systems and what they reveal about the collective thinking of discrete cultures, I knew that looking at the Tibetan and Navajo languages would give me a window into worlds about which I knew very little in this lifetime. In addition to working on my Tibetan writing exercises, I began listening to Navajo language learning tapes.

It was very tough going for me. Suffering as I was from the brain fog associated with toxic exposure, as well as the process of detoxification, I had a hard time drawing conclusions about the two languages. Printed Tibetan is Sanskrit. Each symbol can be pronounced in one of several ways, changing the meaning completely. The swirling symbols of cursive Tibetan were beyond my abilities. I managed finally to learn greetings, thank you, and the names of simple words such as "water," "mother," "father," and so on. I had the same luck with Navajo. While I had studied Latin in high school and had mastered its inflectional nature, the inflectional system in Navajo defeated me. *Okay. For some reason I need to at least familiarize myself with these languages. Maybe more will come to me.*

It was also at this time that I had the opportunity to get to know our neighbors. Living in a mountain community where groups of neighbors share well water and roads are maintained through community funds requires communication and cooperation. Through issues related to the maintenance of the water system we shared with three other households, the first people I met were the manager of our water group, Stu Millendorf, and his wife, Sheila. They were our first friends in the community, and it was through them that Roger and I met the other members of our water group and then people throughout the community. When we eventually became members of the homeowners' association, they would encourage me to serve on the community board. In the meantime, it was wonderful for me to have friends nearby.

In September, knowing we would need to establish a relationship with a local physician, I called Dr. Erica Elliott, one of the authors of *Prescriptions for A Healthy House*, whose practice is in Santa Fe and to whom I had been referred by Susi, the first person I had met at Dr. Rea's clinic. Dr. Elliott was board-certified in both environmental medicine and family practice and highly recommended. When I first called to see if she was accepting new patients, she told me she was not. Then in a curious turnaround that would have a direct impact on a future healing path I would follow, she called me back to tell me that she had decided to make room for me in her schedule. We set an appointment, and at the scheduled time I arrived at her home office.

As with the healers in Dallas, the physician I met that day was not only highly competent and thoroughly knowledgeable in her fields of expertise, she was also intuitive and compassionate. I had prepared a medical history and a list of the antigens I was taking. I also made copies of pages from my rotational diet diary. We spent the next hour discussing my medical history and establishing a patient-doctor relationship. Over time, that relationship would turn into friendship. Moreover, our first meeting set into motion a series of events that would lead me to healers in the heart of the Navajo Nation.

Connectedness

Since I was alone so much, I spent a great deal of time in meditation. To be more precise, I practiced "being present," essentially what Eckhart Tolle discusses in *The Power of Now* and what Deborah Singleton had been encouraging me to do. Each morning I set the intention to be present to what I was feeling in every moment. Coupled with what I had learned in Dallas about staying attuned to my body and taking responsibility for monitoring my thoughts to keep positive energies around me, this attempt to be present in every moment opened a critical door to understanding the concept of "connectedness" with others through our energy fields as well as our thoughts, which are, in essence, a form of energy. Reducing this concept to simple terms, one might think of it as follows. How many times have we heard people say: "I was just thinking of her when the phone rang and it was she calling me to say hello."? Or: "I was seated in a restaurant waiting for my companion to arrive when suddenly I had a funny feeling. I looked up to see someone staring at me from across the room." Anyone who is sensitive to energy movement knows this kind of interaction to be an exchange of energies, and distance is no obstacle to the exchange. The more I meditated to access my higher self, or soul, the more I was able to recognize this kind of energetic communication. I started to perceive myself as not separate from other people. And my consciousness opened even more. With Deborah's encouragement, I sat in stillness with the intention of getting to know more of the healing energies around me.

"Try to identify more of the guides around you. Ask them to come forward and see if you can feel differences in their energies."

As with my first attempts at meditation, my first few attempts to identify and distinguish among the energies of the guides around me were frustrating. Little by little, however, as soon as I felt a presence wishing to communicate, I would know who it was. Angels and soul guides from healing realms came forward to guide me through the dark nights and the processing of past-life memories. I was surrounded by teachers.

One day, sitting in meditation, I felt a familiar presence. *I know you.*

Yes. I am your guardian.

You are the doorkeeper guardian Christine told me all souls have when they come to earth?

I am.

I don't know your name.

You will remember.

Christine said that all other energies of light come to a soul through the soul's doorkeeper.

Correct.

All of the guides and angels have been coming to me through you? They have.

Can I speak to you whenever I want to?

I am always with you.

My friend Christine Gregg is a pipe carrier and sweat lodge keeper. She calls herself a Spirit communicator. She had been talking to me about Spirit and soul since I met her in New Orleans when she came to visit my sister. During a Spirit reading, Christine foretold of my visit to Texas and of my meeting with a wise woman who was to guide me. At the time, I was skeptical of everything she told me. Of course, after meeting Deborah, that skepticism had turned to belief. Now, Christine was also helping to guide me through the transformation I was experiencing.

Setbacks

Fall was ending and the semester drawing to a close, when one morning as Roger was getting ready to leave for his office at Tulane, he slipped as he stepped out of the bathtub. Falling to the tile floor, he dislocated his right clavicle, and stitches were required to close a wound to his head. All that morning, I had an uneasy feeling about Roger, and when he didn't call me, I tried to reach him at his office. It was not until I heard from a friend that he was at the Tulane Hospital emergency room that I knew what had transpired. He wrapped up his affairs at Tulane with his arm in a sling and made arrangements for his office furniture and books to be moved to Santa Fe.

We began our life together as retirees in December 2003 with a trip to the emergency room of our local hospital. On the evening of December 16, I suffered another excruciatingly painful esophageal spasm related to gastro-esophageal reflux disease (GERD). Since symptoms of esophageal spasm are very much like those of a heart attack, the Tulane Hospital emergency physicians in New Orleans had advised me, in each occurrence, to call for help and go to a hospital. Roger called 911 and luckily one of our neighbors in our mountain community was on duty with our local fire and rescue team that night. Our roads were covered with snow and ice, and he knew that only a four-wheel drive vehicle would get up our mountain roads. Much to our surprise, given our location, the rescue team was at our door within 15 minutes in a large SUV. Given my age and symptoms, I was treated as a possible heart attack victim and taken down the mountain to the waiting ambulance and then to our local hospital. At the hospital after a check of cardiac enzymes and an EKG revealed nothing sinister, I was treated for esophageal spasm with the usual tranquilizing drink. I was advised to see my doctor and left with a prescription for cimetidine.

Once home, I called Dr. Elliott for advice and made an appointment to speak to Dr. Rea about my visit to the hospital.

Dr. Elliott agreed to write another prescription for me should I need more cimetidine, but she also asked me to try some natural herbs, teas, and aloe vera liquid for the esophageal burning I was experiencing. She advised me that they could help, but I might be sensitive to them. On my next visit to Whole Foods, I bought the natural remedies and systematically tested each one over the next week. Because of my sensitivities, I was not able to tolerate any of them. During a telephone consultation with Dr. Rea, he asked me if I had tested the peptide antigens. I told him that I had not, and he urged me to do so. Roger and I made plans to visit the clinic when he was able to drive again. In the meantime, my diet was restricted to very bland foods, eaten in food family rotation, and water. Despite medication and a special diet, the burning continued and my appetite diminished. I started losing weight.

13 HEALING CHANGES

February 2004 through May 2004

In February 2004, when Roger was able to drive again, we headed for Dallas so I could test the peptide antigens. Testing revealed sensitivity to some of my own naturally occurring gastric neurotransmitters, or peptides, a not uncommon consequence of exposure to toxins. I began treatment with peptide antigens. After a few weeks, I noticed a diminution in the frequency and duration of bouts of burning. In a few months I gradually returned to the diet I had been following before the esophageal spasm and stopped taking cimetidine. I would continue the peptide antigens for the next eighteen months, after which I would gradually wean off them. I can now eat whatever I want without consequences. No burning, no reflux. I take no medications. If anyone had told me when I was living in New Orleans and under treatment for GERD that one day I would be free of this illness, I would never have believed it. I was under the care of very competent physicians in New Orleans. They were working, however, within the confines of their disciplines, using the time-honored approach of treating GERD symptomatically. My reflux symptoms disappeared after I took antigens for my own gastric neurotransmitters as well as for all of the foods and toxins to which I was sensitive. As my body was responding to the antigen treatment, I supported the desensitization process by clearing the bio-energetic resonance of this illness from my energy fields. I used meditation, intention-setting, and the visualization practices I had been taught in Dallas.

Diminishing EMF Sensitivity

While we were in Dallas, I made several visits to the Arasini Foundation for energy treatments and consultation about my diminishing EMF sensitivity. I had been noticing that I could speak on the phone for longer periods without feeling electrical energy in my body. I wasn't bothered by the electromagnetic fields of running appliances. I began to think that I might be able to start using a computer again and, quite possibly, resume working as a writer and editor. Deborah confirmed my thoughts.

"Your toxic load has decreased enough to allow your energy patterns to become more stable. Don't rush things. Limit yourself to five minutes on the computer the first time you use it. Do your EMF-clearing exercise. Three days later, use the computer for ten minutes. Remember to clear your fields. Just build up your tolerance gradually."

Roger and I also consulted Dr. Rea, who made several recommendations. Following his advice, we bought an ultra-thin, flat screen monitor, which emits weaker electromagnetic fields than a conventional box type monitor, and long cables so that the CPU could be placed far from where I would be sitting and the keyboard could be placed at a comfortable distance from the CPU. We allowed the equipment to outgas for a week in the sun before assembling the system and booting it up.

The process of accustoming my energy fields to the computer's electromagnetic fields took a few months. I began by setting the intention that I was healthy enough to return to working on a computer. My first session on the computer was limited to five minutes. Then I did not use the computer again for three days. The second session was limited to ten minutes, and again I waited three days. I gradually worked up to twenty minutes on the computer at three-day intervals and stayed at that level for three weeks. After that, I reduced the number of days between sessions and gradually increased my time on the computer. Before and after using the computer, I worked with my energy fields, making sure I was grounded, checking the flow in energy pathways, and releasing any energy I retained at the end of each session—following assiduously the instructions I had received at the Arasini Foundation. The biggest problem I encountered was the desire to jump right back to spending hours on the computer, as I had done when I was working full time in the field of public health. Having been warned against doing this, I disciplined myself to follow the suggested program. I'm so glad I did. Today, I am right back where I was before I unmasked for EMF sensitivity, spending as much time as I need to write and do research on the Internet.

Regeneration

In April 2004 I took my first real step into the world I had left. With Roger's help I began driving to Albuquerque to read archival information at the Center for Southwest Research at the University of New Mexico. Another Dallas vision had focused my attention on Barboncito, a Navajo headman, who had played a crucial role in the Long Walk of the Navajos in the 1860s. I planned my trips to coincide with Roger's consulting and teaching trips. He would drive us to the airport in Albuquerque when he was traveling. Then I'd drive to the UNM campus, only ten minutes away. Afterwards, I'd drive back to Santa Fe. I would take a sauna upon returning home, monitor my energy fields, and do grounding and releasing exercises. Of course, before my first visit I had requested information on the environment of the Zimmerman Library where the CSWR is housed. Finding that the carpeting had been laid seven years earlier and there had been no recent renovations or painting, I thought I could chance a visit. I knew I was risking exposure to scented individuals. I had begun noticing, however, that although being near a scented person was still uncomfortable for me because of my exquisite sense of smell, I was no longer having asthma attacks or feeling that my throat was tightening when exposed to scents.

Later in the same month, we hosted the annual meeting of our homeowners' association. The meeting announcement, which was prepared by Sheila, my new friend from our water-sharing group, requested that our neighbors not wear cologne or aftershave to the meeting. We asked that this precaution be taken because scent lingers in the air after scented individuals have been in a room. It is one thing to be exposed to scent while out somewhere, it is another to have scent linger in the air in one's house. We became active members of the association as of this meeting, and this was made possible by our neighbors' willingness not to wear scents at the meetings. This simple courtesy allowed us to integrate ourselves into the life of the neighborhood.

Fear

Right around this time, as I was making breakfast one morning, I realized that I had been abstaining from coffee for about four months following the esophageal spasm in December. I had been introduced to coffee at a young age, and if there was any one thing I associated with the comforts of home, it was coffee. As I sat in my kitchen trying to decide if I could chance a cup, a thought came into my mind: *Have the coffee with milk.*

Milk? What about the lactose intolerance?

You've cleared it.

I have?

You have. Trust your guidance.

My thoughts started to race. *I've avoided milk since I was nineteen years old. I tried to return milk to my diet in New Orleans. That resulted in a bad case of thrush. Is this my highest truth?*

It is.

I wanted coffee so badly that I could not trust my guidance in that moment. I dismissed my longing.

During my next trip to Whole Foods, as I walked past the dairy case, which I generally avoided, my guidance came through strongly: *You can have milk.*

Really?

Really, Jennie.

This time I acted on my guidance. I bought a small container of organic milk. The next morning I tested coffee (organic, of course) and the milk. It was more than a test of foods. It was a test of intuition and trust. Deborah had told me that the more I trusted my guidance, the stronger it would become. And my trust was about to be sorely tested. I had a half cup of coffee with some milk. About forty-five minutes later, I felt a little burning right above the solar plexus.

Oh, no. What am I feeling? Is it the coffee?

Not the coffee, Jennie.

Is it the milk?

Not the milk.

What is it then?

You know what it is. Let it come forward. Don't suppress the answer.

Fear?

Yes. Every illness in the physical body has an energetic imprint. Part of what holds that imprint in place is fear.

What do I do?

You know what to do.

I used one of the clearing visualizations I had been taught in Dallas, the EMF reversal exercise, which also clears negative energies from the energy fields. I called the light to me, seeing a column of light above me and bringing that light in through my crown chakra. I sent it through me to the earth, asking first if Mother Earth would accept what I was sending down. I reversed my circular energy and waited. The burning stopped. I normalized my circular flow.

When I first began meeting other people with environmental illness, I noticed that they exhibited signs of what psychologists refer to as a state of "hypervigilance," which the Merriam-Webster Medical Dictionary defines as "the condition of maintaining abnormal awareness of environmental stimuli." It is one of the key symptoms of post-traumatic stress disorder. Reflecting on my own practice of avoidance, I thought: *After being sickened by the environment and forced into practicing avoidance, how could anyone with EI fail to become hypervigilant? Could the initial realization that something in the environment had sickened me have created the conditions for me to become hypervigilant? Have I been holding fear in my energy fields all this time?*

To me, the answers were clear. I *had* been traumatized. I *had* become hypervigilant. I *was* holding fear in my energy fields. A clearing visualization had stilled the reaction I experienced after drinking coffee with milk. I set the intention to work on releasing the fear underlying my illnesses and the fear of further exposure every day. I was learning to recognize the effects of an emotion held in the energy fields on the physical body. The treatment program at the EHC-D had lessened my sensitivities. I was holding, however, the energetic imprint of fear in my energy fields related to the effects foods and other substances had had on me.

From this point on, I questioned my body's intelligence every time I started to experience a reaction in the physical body. It was hard work, but eventually I learned that I was experiencing fewer reactions to allergens. I started to let the fears go. Besides working on the fear underlying the illnesses and the fear of exposure, I worked also to release the fear associated with my heightened sense of smell. Many people with environmental illness develop a heightened sense of smell, which practitioners consider part of the body's response to chronic exposure to toxins. As an awakening soul with a heightened sense of hearing and sensitivity to my own energies, as well as to the energies of other people, I began to view my sense of smell in a more positive light. I started to associate outgassing body odors with illness or dysfunction. My heightened sense of smell became another of my awakened senses. I no longer believed that every-thing I could smell intensely would harm me. Of course, as my sense of smell became even more sensitive, I chose not to remain in contact with many sources of scent simply because I did not wish to smell certain scents intensely. By accessing inner guidance, however, I could distinguish between the harmful and the simply annoying odors as well as recognize when an odor was imparting information about another person's health. I began to believe what Dr. Rea had said to me at our first meeting, namely, that I would become completely well.

Arizona

In May we traveled to Phoenix, Arizona, to attend my son's graduation. Colin was to be awarded master's degrees in business administration and international management from Arizona State University's W.P. Carey School of Business and the American Graduate School of International Management (now known as the Thunderbird School of Global Management), respectively. Driving, we left Santa Fe three days before the graduation. Stopping overnight in Flagstaff, we stayed in the newer wing of a hotel. Having called the hotel beforehand and expressed my desire for a room that had not been newly painted, carpeted, or treated with pesticides, I was dismayed. I asked that we be moved to the older wing, but there were no other rooms available. The smell of outgassing from the new carpeting, furniture, and linens was very strong. I knew intuitively that one night in this room would not harm us, but the intense smell was difficult to endure. We spent an uncomfortable night there, rising early and leaving as soon as possible. When we arrived on the outskirts of Phoenix, we checked into an older hotel. Our room was a suite with a kitchen, and we were comfortable there.

On the morning of the graduation, we drove to the ceremony early and found seats toward the back of the auditorium and away from most of the audience. I did not want to be near anyone scented so as not to be distracted during the ceremony. As we sat there waiting for the opening procession, I suddenly remembered a remark Deborah had made to me months earlier in response to questions I had asked about my increasing sensitivity to the energies of other people and my heightened sense of smell, which at the time I was finding truly annoying.

"One day you'll be in a crowded theater, and scented people will be all around you. Instead of being disturbed by the scent of a woman near you, you will feel her sadness."

Well, I thought to myself, *if that ever comes to pass, there will be no one more surprised than I!*

14 NAVAJO COUNTRY

August 2004 through December 2004

In August 2004, Christine Gregg came to stay with us for a few weeks. A member of the Katala Okolakiciye (a traditional Lakota women's society), she had just attended the annual Lakota Sun Dance. She and I decided to visit Navajo country to explore some sacred sites and to see firsthand where the Long Walk had taken place. We lugged an air cleaner, bottled water, sheets, pillows, towels, organic food, and my antigens to the Holiday Inn in Chinle, Arizona, outside of the Canyon de Chelly, the main focus of our visit. I had spoken to the manager before booking the room to make sure it had not been recently painted, treated with pesticides, or had new carpeting installed.

My stay at the Holiday Inn was my third in a "normal," that is, non-environmentally friendly, hotel room since I had begun treatment for the pesticide exposure. I could smell everything that was outgassing in the hotel—the cleaning products used on the carpeting, the bed linens, the air freshener used in the hallways. We aired out the room as much as we could by opening the sliding glass door to the patio outside the room and running the air cleaner when the door was closed. Although the outgassing odors were intense, I did not have an asthma attack or develop a headache.

After breakfast we left with a Navajo guide for a jeep tour of the Canyon de Chelly, where Barboncito and his family had lived. Having read several versions of Colonel Christopher (Kit) Carson's entrance into the canyon and of his scorched earth campaign against the Navajos, I was very eager to see the imposing walls of the canyon on top of which the Navajos had taken refuge from Carson and his soldiers. While our guide was somewhat knowledgeable of these events, he couldn't or wouldn't answer my questions about Barboncito and his family. I was hopeful, though, that I would eventually meet someone who could and would.

Shortly after Christine returned home, I called Dr. Elliott and asked to see her for a brief visit at the end of her office day. A few months earlier, she had shared with me her journal, describing her experiences as a teacher in a Bureau of Indian Affairs school in Chinle for Navajo children. I proposed an exchange to her. In return for accompanying me to Chinle, taking me to visit the sites familiar to her from her days as a BIA teacher, I would provide editing for her journal, which she was planning to rewrite for publication, in an hour-for-hour exchange. In addition, I would pay the expenses of the trip. She agreed, and we selected a weekend in early November.

While I was making arrangements for our trip, Dr. Elliott called me and asked if I would contact Adam Teller, a Navajo storyteller who conducted tours into the Canyon de Chelly. She had just attended a book signing at a local retailer and had spoken with the author, who recommended him highly. I called Adam, and we talked about my reasons for wanting to see the canyon again. He asked me what I wanted to learn most. When I told him that I was most interested in seeing anything to do with Barboncito, there was a brief silence, and then he said: "How is it that you have called the great-great-great-grandson of Barboncito?"

I was speechless and delighted at the same time. I booked a tour with him.

A New Patient

It was around this time that the diarrhea Roger had been experiencing for most of his life became severe, and he started to lose weight again. As the symptoms worsened, he began to suspect that he had celiac disease. I looked up the diet for celiac disease on the Internet, and together we developed a food plan for him to follow. The diet did not help. One by one he eliminated foods from his diet until he could eat only six foods that did not send him rushing to a restroom. We had already scheduled a trip to Dallas to be present for my father's heart surgery in October, and I had made an appointment to consult with Dr. Rea about continuing post-menopausal symptoms. Roger accompanied me to that appointment, during which Dr. Rea suggested I test for sensitivities to estrogens and other hormones. Toward the end of the consultation, I mentioned Roger's symptoms.

Turning to Roger, Dr. Rea said: "I wondered how both of you could have breathed in the pesticide dust but only one of you was affected. Let's get you tested for celiac disease, but in the meantime, you should test for food allergies."

While we waited for the results of the test for celiac disease, Roger tested for food allergies. When the testing uncovered allergies to many foods, the scope of the testing was broadened to include allergies to trees, grasses and weeds. He was found to have sensitivities to those substances as well. In the meantime, the test results for celiac disease were found to be negative. We were discovering that Roger had not escaped the effects of the pesticides that had sickened me. His symptoms had just taken a longer time to manifest. Given his continued exposure to type II pyrethroid pesticides in New Orleans during the time he continued to live there after I had left and on his return trips to teach special courses after his retirement, they were not surprising. To my great sadness, Roger entered the EI world, and he would have a long road to healing. Over the next two years, we would return to Dallas for additional testing and follow-up, now not just for me but for him as well. In time, we would discover that sensitivity to book mold was a contributing trigger for his lifelong diarrhea. Roger began Dr. Rea's treatment program, following an organic rotational diet and using antigens. Having tested sensitive to estrone, as well as to other hormones, I added hormone antigens to my antigen schedule.

Canyon de Chelly Vision

In November, Dr. Elliott and I left for Chinle early on a Friday morning, heading south on Interstate 25 and then west on Interstate 40, arriving in Chinle in the late afternoon. Along the way we shifted to a first-name relationship. We stopped at the BIA school where Erica (Dr. Elliott) had taught 30 years ago, before attending medical school, and spoke with the people we met there. We found the tract apartment where she had lived at the time, took a few photos, and checked in at the Holiday Inn. The next morning our guide, Adam Teller, the Navajo storyteller and descendant of Barboncito, picked us up at 9:00 a.m. On the way into the canyon, Adam gave me permission to record what he would tell us that day, so I was able to capture on tape the oral history he would relate about the people who had lived in the Canyon de Chelly from the earliest known inhabitants, the Anasazi, to the present day inhabitants, twenty-first century Navajos. Most important to me, of course, would be the information he would share about his ancestor Barboncito.

I was not disappointed. From the moment we began driving away from the hotel toward the canyon, Adam shared information about the land and the people who had lived there, drawing not only from his education in anthropology but also from his rich knowledge of Navajo oral history. He began with stories about Garcia's Trading Post in Chinle, on the site of which the present Holiday Inn had been built. At the imposing entrance to the canyon, he paused to tell us about the meetings between the Navajos and the American troops led by Colonel John Washington in 1849, with tragic consequences for the Navajos. He described the Navajos' strategic retreat in the early 1860s under Barboncito's leadership to Fortress Rock to avoid capture by Kit Carson's men.

After touring the canyon for most of the morning, we stopped near some Anasazi ruins where we met members of Adam's family, including his father, Ben. He greeted us warmly. I got the feeling as we chatted that Erica and I were being welcomed as friends. Before we left to continue the tour, Ben gave us each a photo taken in 1934 of the Antelope House ruins in the Canyon del Muerto.

Adam took us to see Fortress Rock. As I stood looking up at it, suddenly I was on top of it looking down. One of my Dallas visions was intruding into my consciousness.

This is where I was, looking down?

Yes.

I was looking at soldiers?

Yes.

Intense sorrow overwhelmed me, bringing me back to the moment. I looked at my companions. I struggled to contain what I was feeling. *Help me. I don't want to cry in front of them.*

Surround what you are feeling with light and send it out.

We left after breakfast the next day to return to Santa Fe, and I marveled at the turn of events that had led me to establish a relationship with my travel companion. She spoke Navajo and had been able to joke with the people we had met on the trip, which, of course, made for warm welcomes from everyone. Even more important, her suggestion that I call the Navajo storyteller, Adam Teller, to book a tour had led me to descendants of Barboncito.

In December 2004, Erica let me know that she had just met a Jungian analyst, Jerome Bernstein, who had worked on projects for the Navajo Nation and established relationships with Navajo medicine men. Was I interested in meeting him? Of course the answer was yes, and she put us in touch by e-mail.

Further Healing

Later in December, while shopping at Whole Foods, I suddenly had an overwhelming desire for an apple. I had not eaten fruit since 1988 after adopting Dr. William Crook's anti-candida diet in the hope of lessening recurrent yeast infections. As I stood looking at the organic apples, the thought occurred to me that I had not had a yeast infection since entering treatment at Dr. Rea's clinic.

This desire is not an accident?

Correct.

I can eat an apple?

Yes.

I bought an organic apple. Later that night after dinner, I eyed my prize, a Red Delicious apple. I had not eaten fruit for so many years that my mouth was watering.

I can really eat this?

Yes. Introduce fruit gradually.

I cut off a quarter of the apple and savored every bite. Four days later, I had another quarter. A week later I ate half an apple. Over the next two months I would put every variety of fruit back into my diet in rotation until I was eating a serving of fruit every day. Today I eat two to three servings of fruit a day, generally with nuts or nut butters, with all of the benefits that fruit has to offer and none of the health consequences related to yeast infections or reactive hypoglycemia.

Thought as Energy

Throughout 2004 I continued my practice of "being present" in every moment. From early morning meditation to evening prayer of gratitude for another day, I attempted to be attuned to my body and in touch with my body's intelligence. I continued to monitor my thoughts for negativity and check my energy flows, grounding myself more and more as I opened to the energies around me. Gradually, I began to understand how monitoring my thoughts was helping my overall well-being. Each of us lives through a script we write from the time we are born until the time we die. Our experiences and our feelings about those experiences influence, some might say even *determine*, the thoughts that flow through our minds. Taken together, experiences, feelings, and thoughts create not only the persona with which we show ourselves to the world but also the underlying self or soul that has come to earth for growth. By tuning in to the constant flow of thoughts through my mind, I was beginning to understand the script of my life. Most thoughts come and go in an instant, and more often than not, we are barely conscious of them. Thoughts, however, are a form of energy, and energy in any form affects our energy fields, which in turn affect the physical body. To determine how my thoughts were affecting my body, I started to pay attention to their content. To my surprise, I found that many of them, like my reactions to allergens to which I was no longer sensitive, were fear-based. I came to understand that those fear-based thoughts were putting my body into a "fight or flight," or hypervigilant, state several times a day, stressing the many systems in the body meant to work harmoniously. To counteract this stress, I set the intention that I would recognize my fear-based thoughts whenever they occurred. At each occurrence, I used the visualization Deborah had suggested to me to monitor my thoughts for negativity. I visualized a column of light above my head. I enveloped the fear-based thought with light and grounded it, that is, I sent it through my body, surrounded by light, and into the earth after asking Mother Earth to accept it.

While thought as energy and the monitoring of negative thoughts may be novel to Western-educated readers, those concepts are familiar to many non-Western thinkers. As Buddhists, Tibetans, for instance, take responsibility for monitoring their thoughts so as not to incur the karma associated with adding negative thoughts to the collective consciousness of humanity. Peter Gold in his *Navajo & Tibetan Sacred Wisdom: The Circle of the Spirit* explains that, "Tibetans live in a reality spider-webbed by a complex network of aboriginal and Buddhist forms and ideas that are woven together by intelligence and imagination. Through deep contemplation and rational investigation, the Tibetans have unveiled a vital truth concerning our place in reality: all beings (divine and ordinary) are interconnected by means of the awareness and energy of mind and body." Navajos, like Tibetans, recognize no divide between the sacred and the secular. They believe (according to Carl N. Gorman, the first director of the Office of Native Healing Sciences of the Navajo Nation, as quoted by Jerome Bernstein in his *Living in the Borderland: The Evolution of Consciousness and the Challenge of Healing Trauma*) that "everything originates in thought ... thought is energy ... and it is the energy that molds our environment." The more I was able to "be present" the more I was able to monitor the thoughts as energy, or "thought forms," that were defining my energy fields and to clear the energies of negative thoughts from my fields.

15 NEW HEALING PATHWAYS

February 2005 to June 2005

In February 2005 we returned to Dallas for Roger to have additional testing. While we were in Dallas, I visited the Arasini Foundation for several energy balancing treatments and spoke to Deborah about the painful spinal energy releases and emotional catharses I was continuing to have. She urged me to find an energy healer in New Mexico.

"There are so many advertisements for energy healers in the Santa Fe newspapers," I said. "How will I know whom to call?"

"You will know," she said simply.

Outside of those painful energetic releases and emotional catharses, I was beginning to feel better and better, and it seemed that the sensitivities for which I had been receiving treatment since the fall of 2002 were dissolving. We drove back to Santa Fe with additional antigens for Roger and a mission for me, namely, to find an energy healer with whom to work close to home.

A Proposal

In the meantime, after exchanging several e-mails with me, Jerome Bernstein, the author of *Living in the Borderland* and the Jungian analyst to whom Erica had introduced me by e-mail, asked to meet me. We decided on a lunch meeting at the Cloud Cliff Café and Bakery on a weekday in mid-March 2005. As with all of the people who appeared to accompany me on my healing journey, the man I met was an extraordinary individual. A very tall man—he had told me I would know him because he would be the largest person in the room—Jerome nevertheless exuded an air of gentleness I had sensed in very few people. He asked me about my chemical sensitivity and told me he had been working with environmentally sensitive patients. He had included a chapter on environmental illness in his book—referenced above—that was to be released later in the year. We talked through the next hour about my research on Barboncito, my healing path, the Navajo medical model, and my interest in observing healing through that model. I knew there would be barriers to observing another patient's healing ceremonies. The *hataałi* (Navajo "singer," medicine man or woman) would have to be willing to have me there, and the patient would also have to give permission.

"Jennie, would you like to receive healing through a Navajo ceremony?" Jerome's question interrupted my thoughts.

I heard myself saying, "Yes."

The idea that I would pursue healing through the Navajo medical model had not occurred to me before this meeting. At that moment, however, I knew this was where my healing path was taking me.

"I'll speak to a Navajo *hataałi* I've known for many years and respect greatly. I'll get back to you by e-mail."

I found out later from Erica that I had misunderstood the reason for the meeting. She and Jerome had discussed earlier a collaborative effort to bring healing to patients through Navajo ceremonies and she was referring me to him as a possible "test case."

An Angel of Light

While making the arrangements to meet Jerome, I had also been scouring the ads in the local papers, hoping to find an individual or group that might do the kind of energy balancing done at the Arasini Foundation. One day, quite by chance, I happened to glance at a rack of flyers at our local gas station, and the words "energy balancing" leapt out at me from one of the flyers. I picked up the flyer and turned it over to see a photo of the energy healer advertising her work. The face looking out at me from that photo seemed so familiar that at first I thought I had met her somewhere in Santa Fe. On second thought, I knew I had not, but the feeling of familiarity stayed with me, nevertheless. When I got home, I read the flyer carefully and called the telephone number listed on it. After speaking to the person who answered the phone, Maya Page, I knew that I had not glanced at those flyers accidentally. I was being directed to someone with whom I was intended to work.

On the day of my first appointment, I drove to Maya's house, following the directions she had given me. When I rang the doorbell, the door was opened by a woman whom Christine would later describe as an "Angel of Light." If angels in human guise are sent to hold our hands and walk with us during the difficult times of our soul's journeys through life on earth, then I was blessed that day, as I have been blessed every day of this healing journey through the people who have walked it with me.

I felt very safe in Maya's house. Can you imagine what "feeling safe" means to someone who has been poisoned by the environment? Although I was no longer reacting to substances the way I had two years earlier, I was still working to release the fear of exposure. I could smell nothing outgassing in her house, and the house was older than the seven-year outgassing period for most construction materials. She used non-toxic cleaning products, and most important of all, the laundry detergent she used, Seventh Generation Free and Clear®, was the same one we used. Her home was unscented and so was she. I could relax.

We had a lengthy interview. In answers to my questions, Maya told me about her background, which included fifteen years of study in energy balancing therapies, including time devoted to *Reiki* and VortexHealing®. First and foremost, however, she described herself as an intuitive healer. Given my own experiences as an awakening soul, I felt a common bond with her. I described the energy work and instruction I had received at the Arasini Foundation and gave her as accurate a picture as I could of where I thought I was in the healing process. Maya explained how she worked and told me she could not promise healing in my physical body. She would work with me on an energetic level to encourage the body's natural healing processes to continue. I signed a statement confirming I understood and giving permission for my body to be touched, as I had done at the Arasini Foundation. The work we began on this day would unfold over the next few years, exploring deeper dimensions of my energy systems than, at that time, I knew existed. A few months later, I would take classes from Maya.

Navajo Healing Trail

Over the next two months, e-mails flew back and forth between Jerome, Erica, and me as Jerome collected more and more information about the sensitivities for which I was taking antigens. He was weighing those sensitivities against the exposures I might encounter during a ceremony in a *hogan*, a log and mud plaster shelter in which until the twentieth century most Navajos lived (and many still do) but which now were mainly used for ceremonial purposes. At that point, I had been taking my antigens and following Dr. Rea's treatment program for two and one-half years, and I was ready to let go of my fears of exposure. I e-mailed Jerome. He called me with the telephone number of Johnson Dennison, the *hataałi* who had agreed to speak to me. I called him. He explained that I needed to see a Navajo diagnostician, who would recommend the appropriate ceremony. Only after the diagnostician's determination would he know if he could conduct a ceremony for me. He did not have to explain further. Medicine men and women specialize in certain ceremonies. No one person could possibly know the entire body of ceremonial knowledge, which is transmitted orally. Johnson referred me to a Navajo crystal gazer, Larry Archie, whom I called to arrange an appointment. Should the crystal gazer recommend one of the ceremonies performed by Johnson, then Johnson would perform the ceremony in a *hogan* in Chinle, the day after my appointment with the diagnostician. After checking with Erica and Jerome, both of whom wished to be present at the ceremony, I suggested a middle weekend in June, which was convenient for Larry Archie and for Johnson Dennison as well.

In May 2005 I learned that a dedication ceremony was to be held at Fort Sumner of the Bosque Redondo memorial, a monument to the Navajos and Apaches who had been imprisoned there from 1863 to 1868. I contacted Erica and asked her if she wanted to attend the ceremony. She said she did, and we arranged to drive together to Fort Sumner on the morning of the ceremony.

We arrived early enough to park and carry folding chairs to the assembly area just outside the entrance to the memorial. As the area filled, we looked through the crowd and eventually spotted Jerome and his wife, Susan. We went over to talk to them, and they directed us to another couple standing a little way off — Johnson Dennison and his wife, Rosemary. We made our way over to them, chatted briefly, and returned to our chairs in time to see a familiar face opening the dedication ceremony. Travis Terry, an uncle of Adam Teller, the Navajo storyteller we had met in Chinle, began playing one of his original flute pieces. The melody wafted over us, and the breeze, which had begun to stir, seemed to rise and fall with every inflection of the mournful tune. The sorrow of that place hung all around us, and I wondered if the spirits of the three thousand who had died there had returned for healing. And it was a time for healing. There were apologies from the U.S. Department of Defense to the Navajo and Apache peoples. There were healing words from the many representatives of the federal and state governments. Senators were present, as were the governor and lieutenant governor of New Mexico. The president of the Navajo Nation was there, as well as a representative of the Apache people. All spoke of the injustices that had been inflicted and the opportunity to move forward through acknowledgement of the pain to a place of healing. The most moving part of the ceremony, one that brought tears to my eyes, was a re-enactment of the Long Walk by Navajos dressed in blankets, like the Navajos of the 1860s who had walked the nearly four hundred miles from Navajo country to Fort Sumner. As I sat there, drinking in the ceremony and observing the crowd, I felt the healing that was taking place within me as well as within all those in attendance. Among the many memories that had rushed into my consciousness during the first healing crisis two years earlier had been memories of the Long Walk. I felt the sorrow of that time, crying out from within me in response to the wailing of the Navajo woman leading the walkers.

Reiki Energy Healing

Two weeks after the dedication of the memorial, I attended a day-long class in *Reiki* energy healing at Maya's house, along with several other women. We had received reading materials about the history of *Reiki*, the anatomy of the physical body in relation to the vortices of energy in the energy bodies, the traditional hand positions used in energy healing, and much more, all of which were to be read before the class. Maya began by reviewing the materials and answering our questions. She explained the process of "initiations" that would take place throughout the day that would help us to "open" energetically so that we could channel healing energies. Most important of all, she spoke to us about the ethical responsibilities and obligations a healer has toward a patient. Having received instruction from the healers at the Arasini Foundation and read several books on energy healing, I was familiar with much of what she said during class. What was surprising to me, however, was the reaction I had to the first "initiation." I became thoroughly nauseated, and the nausea did not lift until after the second "initiation." When the "initiations" were completed, Maya supervised us in the placement of hands on the body in the traditional healing positions, and then we were teamed with a partner to exchange energy channeling. I was filled with awe the moment I felt energy moving through my body and into my partner. Although I had been working with my own energy fields and feeling energies move in my body since my first treatment at the Arasini Foundation, becoming an instrument for energy work was a life-altering experience. Over time, I would come to understand on many more levels what transpired whenever I placed my hands as a healer on another person. At that moment, however, I knew only that energies, which held healing intentions, were moving through me.

16 NAVAJO DIAGNOSES AND FIRST HEALING CEREMONY

June 2005

During the week after the *Reiki* initiations, I prepared for my trip to Chinle to see the Navajo diagnostician. I had arranged to see him on a Friday afternoon, and I was hopeful that my healing ceremony would take place the next morning. I contacted Adam Teller and booked another tour of the Canyon de Chelly with him for the afternoon of the day of the ceremony. I invited Erica's sister Veet, who had expressed a desire to see the canyon, to come with us to attend the ceremony and accompany us on the tour. I prepared gift baskets to present to the diagnostician and to the *hataałi*, shopped for and selected fabric for the altar cloths that would be used during the diagnostic and healing ceremonies, and wrote a statement of my intentions for the healing ceremony.

Diagnostic Ceremony

Early in the morning on the day of my appointment with Larry Archie, I picked up Erica and Veet, and we headed south and then west to the Navajo Reservation, arriving just in time for the appointment. After meeting Larry at the entrance of the Chinle Health Care Facility, we entered a *hogan*-like room at one end of the building. There we were introduced to a nurse who had asked to observe the diagnostic ceremony. I agreed that she could stay along with my companions. I presented an altar cloth and a gift basket to Larry. He began by telling us how he had come to his calling, conveying to us some of his family history. I was to learn that it was usual for Navajo practitioners to relate their background to the patient in story form, presenting their credentials orally in contrast to the Western practitioner's practice of displaying his or her credentials in the form of diplomas on an office wall. Larry opened the ceremony by blessing himself and me. He then asked the others to bless themselves in the same fashion. Everyone present would experience the energies of the ceremony and thus participate in the healing that was to begin that day.

Respecting the belief among many peoples that recording the details of a ceremony may weaken its power, I will not describe in detail what took place. A crystal gazer is one of three types of Navajo diagnosticians, the other two being hand tremblers and listeners. As the name suggests, a crystal gazer looks at crystals at various points in the diagnostic ceremony. Larry asked me a number of questions that led me to believe he could see the past events of my life.

At the end of the ceremony he said, "You need three ceremonies to be entirely well again: the Protection Ceremony, the Wind Way, and the Life Way."

Three ceremonies? I thought to myself. *Can we afford three ceremonies, the travel costs, the lodgings?*

"Does Johnson Dennison do all three of the ceremonies?"

"He does the first two. I do not know who does Life Way."

After we left the health care facility, I called Jerome and Johnson. The first of the healing ceremonies, the Protection Ceremony, was then scheduled for the following morning at nine o'clock. I called Roger to let him know that the ceremony would take place the next morning, and my companions and I prepared to separate. Erica and Veet would be camping outside the Canyon de Chelly, and I had taken a room at the Holiday Inn. They dropped me off and headed for the campgrounds. After dinner, I went to bed.

Protection Ceremony

Early the next morning, Erica and Veet knocked at my door. After a hot breakfast, they showered and changed in my room. Out of respect for what we were about to experience, we dressed in long skirt outfits with appropriately modest tops and Navajo jewelry. We drove to the *hogan* outside the Chinle Health Care Facility, arriving early at 8:30 a.m. We met Jerome in the parking lot. Outside the *hogan* was a *ramada,* a summer shelter usually built with boughs of juniper, cedar, or cottonwood. Much to our surprise, three people were seated under the *ramada.* They introduced themselves as Mary, Peter, and Philip and told us they were waiting to speak to Johnson Dennison. As we chatted, the nurse who had observed the diagnostic ceremony arrived to witness the healing ceremony. When Johnson arrived, we all walked into the *hogan,* turning to the left inside the doorway and walking in clockwise fashion around the perimeter. The threesome we had just met began speaking to Johnson.

Suddenly Erica nudged me. "Isn't Peter the author of the book you gave me?"

"You mean *Navajo & Tibetan Sacred Wisdom: The Circle of the Spirit?*"

"Yes."

As he and his friends turned to leave, I stopped Peter and asked him if he was, in fact, the author of that book. He said he was. I extended my hand to him, telling him what an honor it was for me to meet him, for his book was the very first I had read when beginning my research on Navajo beliefs. We shook hands, and I asked him to wait a moment while I spoke to Johnson. He agreed. I turned to Johnson and asked if I could invite Peter and his friends to my ceremony because I had just discovered a connection with him. Johnson said I could, so I extended the invitation, which was accepted. At that moment, Veet and Philip recognized each other, having met 25 years earlier on the East Coast.

We took our places on cushions set on the floor. Johnson and I sat according to custom on the west side of the *hogan,* with me to his left. The men sat to the right of Johnson on the south side, and the women sat to my left on the north side. I laid out the altar cloth to my right and positioned my gift basket, my statement of intentions, and my offering to one side of the cloth. Johnson began by telling us about himself and how he had come to be a "singer." He outlined the parts of the ceremony and explained how the patient and all those present would participate in the healing through prayer, breath, and movement. I was struck at that moment by the similarities in the approach to healing used by both Navajo healers and energy healers, remembering the affirmation with which Maya opened each healing session, as well as the controlled breathing and the placement of hands for healing both in Santa Fe and at the Arasini Foundation in Dallas. Johnson invited us to pray according to our own religious beliefs, and he encouraged us to invite whomever we wished to be present in the *hogan*.

"If, for instance, you would like Jesus to be present," he said, "then invite Him to be present."

Surprised by the intense feeling I suddenly had that I needed to extend this invitation, I closed my eyes and prayed, asking Jesus to be with us. At that moment I felt a powerful presence, and tears came to my eyes. I felt love, so intense and at the same time familiar, and the familiarity startled me. I did not have time to think about what I was feeling, for I began to see beings of light in the *hogan*, some of whom were dressed in Navajo clothing of the 1860s. I realized that a temporal veil had been pulled back once again. It was difficult for me to process all that I was "seeing" and sensing. The ceremony was beginning, and I focused my attention on the *hataałi*.

Johnson began by blessing himself and me. As he was blessing himself, I noticed that the areas of the body he was touching were close to the chakras or to areas of the body where energy healers place their hands during treatment sessions. Energy healers, for instance, will ground their patients through the soles of the patients' feet. Johnson began by blessing the soles of his feet, moving up the body to his head. After he had blessed me in the same way, he invited the others in the *hogan* to bless themselves. Beginning with the woman to my left, each woman blessed herself in the same fashion. Afterwards, each man blessed himself.

Out of respect for the belief system through which this ceremony was conducted, I will not describe in detail what took place. In general, when a *hataałi* sings over a patient, he or she prays for the patient as part of a collective—the patient within his or her family, the patient within his or her clan or community as well as within the cosmos. Prayers or chants are conducted in series of four, in recognition of the four directions and what each direction symbolizes in the Navajo worldview. The *hataałi* calls upon the Holy Ones, whose stories represent the qualities or energies needed by the patient, to be present. Within the Navajo medical model "dis-ease" or illness is caused by an imbalance within the natural order of things in which human beings are primary players. The patient must be brought into balance within the universe in order to heal. Here, too, there is similarity between the Navajo medical model and the energy healing model. Energy healers work to bring their patient's energy systems back into balance, which allows the body to be receptive to healing. Since energies—those of people to each other and to places, elements, animals, and so on—are connected throughout nature and the universe through what is referred to as the universal energy field, when one person's energy is rebalanced, rebalancing occurs universally.

As the ceremony proceeded, Johnson guided us, speaking in English only when he gave us instructions, for the ceremony was conducted in Navajo. At one point during the prayers, I felt pressure in the soles of my feet. The pressure became intense and painful. It moved from my feet through my legs and into my upper body. When it hit the vortex of energy in my body known as the heart chakra, I started to weep. The energy swept through the upper chakras and out the crown of my head, and I sobbed uncontrollably. It was as if the trauma that had befallen my seven-year-old self had been sucked right out of my body. As I peered through tear-soaked eyes, I could see the child I was, surrounded by a beatific aura of white light. On either side of my child-self stood two beings of white light.

I heard a voice say, "Let her go."

With all the will I could muster, I did. My face was sopping wet. Because I had no tissues with me, I could not wipe my face. Erica, who was seated next to me, reached over and offered me the edge of her dress to wipe my face, an act of kindness I will not forget. When Johnson had finished that series of prayers, he, too, came to my rescue, with tissues. I was able to blow my nose and breathe freely again.

When the ceremony was concluded, I invited Johnson to join us for lunch at the Best Western restaurant. He, however, had to leave immediately for another ceremony. Peter, Philip, Mary, and the nurse were headed to other appointments. Peter invited us to visit him later that night at his *hogan* near the entrance to the Canyon de Chelly. We accepted his invitation, and he gave us directions. The rest of us agreed to meet at the restaurant in an hour's time. In the meantime, Erica suggested we drive along the south rim of the Canyon de Chelly to the overlook for Spider Rock, the home of Spider Woman, a place sacred to the Navajos. There, she said, would be the perfect place for me to pray and express gratitude. We reached the parking area, and Erica and Veet waited while I walked up the trail, alone, to the overlook. Spider Rock juts up hundreds of feet from the floor of the canyon in twin spindles, one slightly higher than the other, framed at a distance by the massive walls of the canyon. I stood there, feeling the power of that mythical formation all around me.

I've lived here.

Yes.

I prayed. *Why am I to know this in this lifetime?*

Healing.

For whom?

You and others.

After walking back down the trail, I called Adam Teller. He, his wife, and one of their children, their eldest son, joined us for lunch. After introductions, we dined on typical Navajo foods, mutton stew, fry bread, and coffee. We were an unusual group—a medical doctor, a Jungian psychoanalyst, a Mensa-level biologist/organic gardener, a writer, and descendants of Navajo headman Barboncito, who had negotiated the release of the Navajos from Fort Sumner—all brought together by grace to heal toward our highest good.

After lunch, Erica, Veet, and I went back to the hotel to change into casual clothes, and Adam collected Jerome and us in his jeep for a tour of the canyon. It was my third trip into the canyon where Barboncito was born, and my second with one of his descendants. As with the last tour, I was invited to record what Adam would tell us so I took out my tape recorder and turned it on.

When the tour was concluded, we said our goodbyes to Adam and Jerome. Erica and Veet returned to their campsite, and I went back to my room to rest. Around 7:30 p.m. we met outside the hotel lobby and drove to Peter's *hogan,* which was a traditional structure enhanced by electricity and running water. It was thrilling for me to be in the home of the author whose insightful analysis of the similarities in the Navajo and Tibetan worldviews had been my first introduction to concepts critical to Navajo and Tibetan thinking. I sat in Peter's hogan, in a dream-like state, knowing that our meeting had not been accidental and wondering what it was we four were setting right on a soul level, even as Peter shared with us some of the experiences he had had in the course of writing his book. The time went by quickly. We said goodnight, thanking Peter for his hospitality and exchanging e-mail addresses with him.

The next morning we drove back to Santa Fe on the first of

four days of reverence I was to maintain following the ceremony. I was eager to see Roger, who had not been well enough to travel with us. Before leaving on my trip, I had prepared meals and frozen them for him. I was happy to see that he had eaten most of the food and seemed to have managed reasonably well while I was gone. He was still having trouble tolerating most foods and was always very tired. After giving him a rundown of what had happened over the weekend, I raised the question of whether we could afford the additional ceremonies. Roger, as usual when it came to anything that could help me, said we'd work it out. Although he was retired and not feeling well, he was still doing consulting work from home, and the money from that work was helping us pay the considerable bills we had run up since our exposure to pesticides. In addition to the isolation one encounters in the EI world, there is the constant worry of how to pay for treatment, much of which is not covered by medical insurance.

Soul Guardian

During the four days following the ceremony, I experienced a body-mind-spirit detoxification, much like the first one I had experienced in Dallas, with rushes of memories into my consciousness, intense emotional catharses, and painful spinal energy releases. One memory, in particular, ripped through my heart chakra with such force that I thought my chest was exploding. I remembered the name of my guardian. It was Jesus. Filled with remorse for turning my back to Jesus when my first marriage ended and living the next twenty-two years of my life in a spiritual wilderness, I wept and wept and wept.

I prayed. *Jesus, I am so sorry. You were with me when I was born?*

I was. I will be with you when you leave.

Why have I become aware of you in this lifetime?

This awareness is part of what you promised to do.

My soul promises? I was remembering the vision of the throne of golden light I had had in Dallas.

Yes. Your soul promises.

I don't remember all of them.

There is a part of you that does remember. You've chosen to walk a certain path in this lifetime. Opportunities to recognize your promises will unfold. Patience, Jennie. Allow things to unfold.

Are you the Jesus of my childhood studies?

Yes...and much more. I am All That Is. And so is humanity. Not everyone remembers that We are One.

All paths lead to God's Truth?

Yes. The Divine is known by many names. When you are ready, when your heart opens, the Divine comes to you.

It was then I knew why I had felt a familiar presence in the hogan. The Christ Consciousness had always been mine. I had just not been fully aware of it. How ironic that I had been brought to this realization through a Navajo healing ceremony within a belief system worlds apart from the belief system in which I had been raised as a child. How typical that grace finds you when you are ready for it. It was no accident that a Navajo ceremony had triggered greater understanding of my spiritual enlightenment. In a dramatic way I had been given confirmation that we—all human beings of varied backgrounds and religious beliefs—are One and that all paths lead to God's Truth.

It was no longer possible for me to look at another human being and to see that person as anything other than a soul reflecting back to me what was within. A universe of experience was mine, if only I could grasp it. I was beginning to understand what the French theologian Teilhard de Chardin had meant when he said that we were "not human beings having a spiritual experience but spiritual beings having a human experience." That understanding, however, did not make me immune to the emotional forces at work on the earth. Time and again I would find myself caught between two realms, where in the secular I was reacting to what was before me, being sucked into an emotional maelstrom, while in the realm of the soul I was a silent witness to the unfolding drama. *When,* I asked myself repeatedly, *will I be able to maintain a soulful equilibrium "that looks on tempests and is never shaken"?* as Shakespeare had described love in his Sonnet 116.

17 SECOND HEALING CEREMONY: WIND WAY

July 2005 through August 2005

A month later, in the middle of July, Erica and I drove together to Chinle, where we stayed the night to rest before the Wind Way ceremony. Early the next morning, we met Jerome at the Best Western restaurant, and the three of us drove to Johnson Dennison's *hogan*, where parts of the ceremony were to be conducted. It was one of those strikingly beautiful mornings in the Southwest, with the sun high in a sky that stretched for miles, clear and blue, over the surrounding mountain ranges. When we reached our destination, Johnson greeted us and invited us to enter his *hogan*. We took our places according to custom. I laid out the altar cloth I had brought with me and placed my offerings to one side.

Johnson began by telling us how he had been called to be a "singer." He then blessed himself and me in the same way in which he had blessed us in the Protection Ceremony, that is, from the soles of the feet to the top of the head. Then he invited my companions to bless themselves. As in the Protection Ceremony, the *hataałi*, during the Wind Way, prays for the patient within his or her collective group to bring the patient into balance in his or her relationships with family, community, nature, and cosmos. While he prayed, he assembled the offerings that represented my family, my community, and my work, which were to be brought with us to the offering site.

At a certain point in the ceremony we left the *hogan* in the order prescribed by custom and got into our Jeep, with Erica driving. Following directions from Johnson, we headed toward huge mesas a mile or so from the *hogan*. The paved road gave way to dirt, and we found ourselves climbing the side of one of the mesas. When we reached our destination, we stopped the

Jeep and walked to an area Johnson selected. There, under the expansive sky with the sun shining and the power of the mesas all around us, Johnson conducted the next part of the ceremony, praying to bring me into balance with the winds. As if on cue, the light breezes that had been blowing intensified, creating a metaphysical connection to the power of the ritual. It seemed as if the four of us had moved into another dimension. I saw the winds come in from the four directions to surround us. Four beings of white light stood north and south, east and west of us, and we were enveloped in the light. We returned to the Jeep and drove back to the *hogan*. There, Johnson concluded the ceremony, telling me, in particular, that my work had been blessed. His words resounded through my energy fields. As an adult, I had come to understand, as most adults do, that the childhood retort to name calling, "sticks and stones may break my bones, but names will never hurt me," was very far from the truth. Words do hurt. And there were many times in my life when I had wished I could scoop something I had said out of the air to lessen its impact. As I felt the affirming energy of the *hataali's* words, I suddenly understood words and communication in a totally new way. It wasn't just the emotional impact of the words on my psyche, it was the energy of the words, specifically, the vibrational rate of that energy, that I was feeling as a sense of harmony within my energy fields and subsequently my body. On the other hand, why can words hurt? Because the dense vibrations of hurtful words upset the balance of our energy fields and remain as wounds to body, psyche, and soul.

Obstacles for Roger

After lunch Erica and I parted company with Jerome and drove back to Santa Fe. We were hurrying to get back before dark for a social engagement Erica was to attend, and I was anxious to find out how Roger had managed while I was away. Upon reaching home, I learned that most of the food I had prepared for him had gone uneaten. He told me that his appetite and his energy had failed, and he seemed to be weaker than ever. As I sat looking at my husband, I wondered if he would consider returning to Dr. Rea's clinic in Dallas to continue his testing. I suspected that not all of his sensitivities had been detected, but I found myself in an area of our relationship where in the past I had always turned to Roger for advice. Roger's path to healing was fraught with obstacles I had not encountered. He had been advised to have his teeth removed because of serious periodontal infection. In a few months, he would begin that process. Further, he is seventeen years older than I, and the body's ability to detoxify decreases with age. Since all I could do was to ask if he was open to more testing, I did. To my relief, Roger agreed a trip to Dallas was warranted. Suffering from fatigue and brain fog, Roger did not feel strong enough to travel to Dallas just then. Over the next two months, as he continued to take his antigens and follow an organic rotational diet, I experimented with preparing foods in several ways, cooking hot meals for him twice a day in the hope of enticing him to eat more. He agreed to see Maya for energy healing. She was to help him regain his appetite through his most intense periods of detoxification, when he would generally stop eating. Several times, we arrived at Maya's house after Roger had had no appetite for two days. Following treatment, he would be able to eat a substantial meal.

Another Healing Crisis

I observed the four days of reverence following the Wind Way, experiencing the same kinds of rushes of memories into my consciousness, emotional catharses, and painful energy releases I had experienced after the Protection Ceremony. Once again, I found myself in the crucible of the dark night of the soul, emerging afterwards even more transformed. The healing crisis following the Wind Way went on for almost six weeks. My visions focused on the dark side of humanity: warfare, genocide, torture, cruelty, from pre-historic times to the present.

Jesus, why am I seeing these events? Why am I feeling them? The pain is so bad.

You are clearing the memories of these events from your energy fields.

Why am I doing this?

Part of the path you've chosen to walk. Allow your path to unfold. This will all pass.

There were days when I thought myself back in Dallas during the initial healing crisis; the pain of the memories coming forward was at times beyond what I thought I could bear. Only now, however, as with the other crises I endured in Santa Fe, I was not alone. As they continued in intensity, I worried about their effects on Roger. More than once, my worry was justified as he addressed me in frustration.

"Don't you think you should call Carol Cole? Ask her if you need medication for depression."

Even though I knew I was in another dark night, I would call Dr. Cole. She urged me to share with Roger more of what I was experiencing, and I began to do so. Whether it was our history together, his experience of my strong, stable personality, or the short recovery periods following the weeping episodes, Roger accepted my explanations with equanimity. If our situations had been reversed, I do not know if I could have done the same thing. His support was vital to my spiritual growth, and for that I will always be grateful.

I turned as well to Maya for energy treatment, and I paid attention to her descriptions of how she was working on my energy fields. Little by little, I learned how to work in the same way to help myself, but very often during the dark nights energy treatment did not lessen the pain. Sometimes the treatments themselves were painful, or they precipitated even more painful releases. Only faith and determination kept me going during these periods.

18 DEEPER LEVEL OF CONSCIOUSNESS

September 2005 through December 2005

In September 2005 we returned to Dr. Rea's clinic. Testing revealed Roger's sensitivity to additional molds and other environmental toxins, and he began taking antigens to lessen those sensitivities. While we were there, I told Dr. Rea that I seemed to have lost my sensitivities to food and colognes and I was no longer experiencing esophageal burning or asthma attacks. I could still smell colognes intensely, but I was not being sickened by them. Dr. Rea suggested I wean myself gradually off the antigens I had been taking since October 2002 and then report to him if symptoms recurred. We returned to Santa Fe, and Roger added sauna detoxification to his healing therapy along with his new antigens. We continued to follow the four-day rotational diet in the hope of lessening his food sensitivities. Over the next six months, I weaned myself off the antigens.

Removal of the Veil

Later in September, I completed Maya's second-level certification class in *Reiki* and continued energy self-treatment. As I continued to clear past-life energies from my energy fields, the vibration of the energies around me changed, and I began to connect with a deeper level of consciousness. My Western-acculturated mind was opening more and more to the sacred in all that was around me but especially to the sacred within me, within us all. Once begun, that opening, or awareness, removes the veil that separates us from the sacred. If one thinks of the sacred as everything within one's vision—and I include in the meaning of the word "vision" thoughts, imagination, and perception—then numinous communication, or mystical experience, becomes possible. The personalities that Jerome Bernstein refers to as "borderland" in his *Living in the Borderland* are people for whom the veil between the secular and the sacred is either very thin or no longer exists. Jerome proposes that it is through three portals—evolution, personality structure, and trauma—that people can cross over into the borderland. I can attest through personal experience to the truth of his vision for at least two of those portals. The first, of course, is trauma, the trauma I experienced as exposure to toxins cut off my access to the world I knew, thrust me into the world of environmental illness, and led me to the energy healers at the Arasini Foundation. There is also the trauma I experienced as a seven-year-old, which lived inside me, locked away from my consciousness, until a "shower vision" brought that memory forward. Long before my trip to Dallas and shortly after the breakup of my first marriage, when I was in my mid-thirties, I had a vision, or a memory, of the molestation when I was taking a shower. In retrospect, I understand that the trauma of the disso-lution of my marriage may have triggered that memory. At the time, however, I was dealing not only with the severing of what I had considered a union for life but also with exclusion from my childhood religion, which does not permit divorce. I gave no further thought to the memory because I did not feel capable of dealing with it as well as the spiritual void I had entered. I had no further visions until over ten years later, again after the breakup of another relationship. I was living in Maryland and working as a writer and editor in the field of public health when the shower visions started again. From time to time during my morning showers I would see future work assignments and places I would visit. One of my shower visions is still vivid. I saw myself in a rectangular room in a large official-looking building. Inside this room was a U-shaped table. I entered the room and took my place at the bottom of the U. I looked around and saw that I was the only woman present. Shortly after having that vision, I was asked to attend a meeting in a large government building in Washington, D.C. Upon entering the conference room, I was surprised to see a U-shaped table. I was directed to my place, which was at the bottom of the U. When all of the attendees had finally arrived and the door was shut, I looked around and realized that I was the only woman present. At the time, I did think the source of these shower visions was intuition, but I had only a vague idea of what that was. I never connected intuition with soul, which of course, I now do.

The second portal through which I crossed into the borderland, which I perceive as the realm of the soul, is the evolutionary process. Jerome describes this process as a reconnection of the Western psyche to nature, in which as an awakening soul I now know I participate. All of nature speaks to me. I see the earth and everything in it and on it as consciousness into which I am sometimes called to enter. On page 82, second paragraph, of *Living in the Borderland* Jerome describes borderland experiences as "direct experiences of transrational reality." In the next paragraph he comments "...reconnection with these nonrational dimensions of reality is taking place rapidly on a collective level within Western culture and is beginning to affect many individuals at all levels of society." The conclusion he reaches is one that I and many others like me share. That leaves, of course, the chicken-and-the-egg question: Which came first? Trauma or the evolutionary process? For me, the path to awakening is clear. My soul journey, or spiritual evolution, began eons ago, and its timing was such that I would awaken with many others during this time of transformation for the earth and humanity. The triggers to my awakening have been traumatic events.

As I continued to meditate and to work on my energy fields and chakras, my inner vision opened even more, allowing me not only to feel blocks in my energy flows but to see them and communicate with them as well. Over time, for instance, and with further guidance from Deborah Singleton, I would learn to see when I was holding a dysfunctional energy pattern somewhere in my body. I could sense if that pattern was related to a belief or to an emotion I was holding. With Deborah's help, I would learn to clear those patterns.

Anchor for Spiritual Growth

I consulted Dr. Cole as I became more and more sensitive to the energies around me. It is so easy to be seduced by the wonder of expanded consciousness and to use it as an excuse for not engaging on the human level. As I came to understand, dealing with the here and now of our human relationships is as crucial to soul development as it is to healing the wounds within. If we are "spiritual beings having a human experience" (Teilhard de Chardin, referenced earlier), we must grapple with the difficulties of relationships both close and casual as we navigate through the human experience. Often, we are in denial about the part we play in the dysfunctional aspects of our relationships or rationalize them as part of the soul's experience on earth. In the psychotherapeutic relationship, I was never allowed to take the mirror away from who I am in relation to the people in my life or to use my spiritual sensibilities to avoid emotional engagement. Over and over, I was prodded to work on issues typical of a woman of my generation who—growing up with the golden rule—had learned how to love and do for others but had never learned to love and honor herself. To be compassionate to others, I was now being told, I had to be compassionate to myself. Speaking my truth in a loving way to honor myself and the divinity within became my focus, and I set my intentions to do so. Roger made me aware of how much time I gave to others while neglecting my writing as well as the things that were important to us and to our relationship. I established work hours, e-mailing family and friends that from Monday through Friday I would take phone calls only in the evenings. That one step allowed me to dedicate myself to writing this book.

Step by step, I was learning how to live in both the secular and the sacred dimensions and to interpret the information that was coming to me. The learning curve was steep. At times, because of my new sensibilities, I felt the pain of others or the disorder within their energy fields so acutely that I dissolved into tears. After one very acute and painful sensing of another person's energies, I called Maya for advice.

"Our first impulse when we feel something like that is to get away from it or to resist it. The best thing to do, however, is to surround those energies with light and send them out to the universe, expressing your thanks for the information."

A little while later, I had the chance to do as Maya had suggested. I was seated near someone in a restaurant when I started to feel the person's unsettled energies. I surrounded those energies with light and sent them out to the universe, expressing my thanks. The reaction in my nervous system faded.

Near the end of 2005, I heard from Jerome that Johnson Dennison had just begun working with Gerald King, a *hataałi* who specialized in Life Way. I was given his telephone number, and I called him to set a date for my Life Way ceremony.

19 THIRD HEALING CEREMONY: LIFE WAY

May 2006 through December 2006

In May 2006, Roger began having the series of oral surgeries that would remove not only all of his teeth but also the underlying bone. Dr. Rea had recommended intravenous (IV) infusions of amino acids, vitamins, and minerals before and after each of the surgeries, performed a quadrant at a time, to mitigate the effects of post-surgical detoxification. It was to be a time of considerable pain for Roger; however, following this period, his gastrointestinal system began to heal. His appetite started to stabilize, and he regained some of the weight he had been losing.

At the end of July, when Roger was in a stable period, I headed to Chinle for my Life Way ceremony with Christine, who had arrived in Santa Fe a few days earlier. When we got to Chinle, we checked in at the Holiday Inn. The next morning, my guests for the ceremony gathered in the parking lot of the Best Western restaurant. They included Christine, Jerome, Maya, and Maya's husband, Michael. Erica was not able to attend because of a last-minute conflict. Christine, Jerome, and I drove to the gas station in Many Farms where we were to meet Gerald King. Maya and Michael followed. A pickup truck pulled up near us and inside was a Navajo man who appeared to be about 45 years old. He introduced himself as the Life Way *hataałi*. We followed him to his property, which was visible from the gas station, and parked near his *hogan*. Outside the hogan three young men were digging a pit. It was about 10:30 in the morning on a very hot day. The pit's resemblance to a grave unnerved me. Jerome must have sensed my unease. He called me aside.

"The shape of the pit sometimes upsets people. How are you feeling about it?"

"Because it resembles a grave?"

"Yes."

"I'm really anxious. I've been dreading this last ceremony ever since Gerald King described it to me months earlier."

"Reflect for a moment on your anxiety. What comes to you?"

I took a deep breath and grounded myself. I focused on my feet. A thought came to me quickly: *Fear of dying.*

Fear of dying?

Jennie, you need to die in order to be reborn.

Jesus?

I am with you.

Death and Rebirth

I knew Jerome was waiting for an answer. I heard the following words come out of my mouth: "I understand now, Jerome. It is fear of dying. This is a rebirthing ceremony. I need to die in order to be reborn. I'm okay. Thank you."

The significance of the name of the ceremony I was about to experience had escaped me to this point. Life Way, with its ritual burial of the patient within the womb of Mother Earth, was not about death but life. I had been called to a new life of spiritual communion, taking me out of the unconscious void in which I had lived my life to a new awareness of the divine and the sacred. Life Way would provide a rite of passage for me as well as complete the circle of Navajo healing, which had begun a year earlier.

We all watched as Gerald King and his helpers built a fire in the now-finished pit. As the fire burned ever higher, Gerald seated himself near us in the shade to rest and told us the story of how he had been called to be a "singer." When he finished speaking, he went back to check the fire. Deciding the pit had been heated sufficiently, he directed the removal of the burning logs. Then the preparation of the womb within the pit began in earnest. When all was ready, he invited my guests to seat themselves on folding chairs in a shaded area and asked me to undress. I removed my ceremonial clothes, storing them in our Jeep while stripping to sauna shorts, tank top, and slip-on shoes. Handing my wedding ring and watch to Christine, I walked to the pit as directed. Slipping off my shoes to one side, I climbed into the bed that had been prepared for me and watched as the womb was sealed with blankets. I lay in total darkness. I felt intense heat rising from beneath me. Within seconds I was drenched with perspiration. I have taken 160-degree saunas, but the heat from those saunas was as nothing compared to the heat in the pit that day. The air was heavy with the scent of steaming herbs and wood, and I began coughing. I could hear Gerald chanting in Navajo, although the sound of his voice was muffled by the blankets. With my physical sight blinded, I relied on inner vision and guidance to comfort me. Although I knew that Jesus was with me, anxiety gripped me. A corner of the blankets was suddenly pulled back, and Gerald thrust a gourd at me.

"Drink as much as you can."

I managed three large gulps of the bitter liquid and handed the gourd back. I lay back down and the pit was sealed once again. I started talking to Jesus. Words and images came into my mind: "safe," "healing," "rebirth." I worried that I would not be able to breathe in enough oxygen to remain alert. That fear was addressed when a corner of the blankets was pulled back briefly, and Gerald asked if I was okay. I greedily gulped the cool air into my lungs before responding, and the womb was once again sealed. I silently thanked Jesus. From time to time over the next hour and twenty minutes, I asked for air when it became difficult to breathe. The heat in the pit was maintained through the application of water to the heated stones and shells beneath where I lay. I could hear the water gurgling out of its container and then hissing when it hit its target. I waited through all of the chants and prayers for the womb to be opened, but it was not. At first, Gerald sang by himself. Then his voice was joined by the other Navajo men present. Gerald began to call out the amount of time

I had been in the womb—45 minutes, one hour. Then the men's voices were joined by those of the Navajo women at the ceremony. I finally realized that the *hataałi*, like a midwife waiting for a child to present itself in the birth canal, was waiting for me to announce that I was ready to be reborn. I asked to come out. The blankets were pulled back, and I quickly shielded my eyes from the light. A canopy had been pulled over the pit, but the light was still too intense for me. Gerald held a ceremonial object for me to grasp. I grabbed it, and he hoisted me out of the pit. I started to sway. He asked one of his helpers to steady me, and the three of us walked toward the *hogan*. My guests and the rest of the helpers followed

Convergence

Christine carried in my altar cloth, gift basket, and offering. We all entered the *hogan* according to custom and took our prescribed places. After everyone was seated, Gerald blessed himself and me. He invited the others to bless themselves, beginning with the woman to my left. He explained that everyone present would participate in the healing of the patient and receive healing in return. He blessed the *hogan*. Then he began the series of prayers and songs that would constitute this part of the Life Way, praying to bring me into balance within my family, my community, and the cosmos. At one point during the ceremony, as had happened during the Protection Ceremony, I felt a powerful force move up from my feet through my body, and I began weeping. Too tired to hold my head up any longer, I put my head down on my chest and sobbed. Scenes from the earlier ceremonies flashed through my mind, and I became oblivious to the other people in the *hogan*. I sensed the nearness of the healing energies that had been present at the first two ceremonies. I saw the angels of light on either side of my child-self as well as the four beings of light standing in the cardinal directions. I felt the energies of Jesus and his love all around me.

A temporal veil had been pulled back, once again, and I saw beings of light, dressed as Navajos would have been in the 1860s. Intense pain suddenly wracked my body, and I called on whatever reserves of strength were left within me not to cry out.

Jesus?

I am here, Jennie. Let it go. You are healing that lifetime.

I let it go. I let it go. I let it go!

After what were to me several heart-stopping moments, the pain was sucked out through the top of my head. My body went limp, and a feeling of peace flooded my body. Gerald closed the ceremony. My companions brought in the food we had packed to share after the ceremony. At that point, I did not think I could stand, and I gratefully allowed my friends to do the unpacking. It was about three o'clock, and I realized that I was ravenously hungry. Given how long the ceremony had been, I was sure everyone else was, too. After eating and drinking some water, I managed to stand and to help with cleaning up. We exited the *hogan* as prescribed. Before parting company with my guests, I presented them with gifts that had been blessed during the ceremony. Feeling much too weak to drive, I asked Christine to drive us back to the Best Western restaurant so Jerome could return to his car. Before leaving, he suggested that Christine and I consider staying another night to rest. We had planned to drive home after the ceremony, but I was obviously too tired to help with the driving. I called Roger to tell him how things had gone and to ask how he was feeling. He said he was fine. He thought it a good idea that we stay another night before attempting the six-hour trip back to Santa Fe. Christine and I checked back in to the Holiday Inn. I took a shower and got into bed. Later that night we went to the Best Western restaurant for dinner and then turned in.

The next morning we left for home, driving the now very familiar route 191 south from Chinle to Ganado, passing isolated *hogans* along the way. Turning east onto 264, we drove through a reseeded Ponderosa Pine forest, the saplings clustered in bunches along the side of the road, and into Window Rock, the seat of the Navajo Tribal Council. There we turned south and headed for Interstate 40 east and home.

More Detox for Roger

When I arrived home, I discovered that Roger had not had an easy time while I was gone.

"Roger, you haven't eaten the meals I prepared for you."

"I spent most of my time in bed. No energy and no appetite."

"You didn't say anything when I called you."

"I didn't want you to worry. You were tired, so I encouraged you to stay another night."

He looks terrible. But that is Roger. He always puts others ahead of himself.

"Roger, will you consider having someone stay with you the next time I go out of town?"

"That's not necessary."

"Until we know that you have stopped having these bouts of detoxification, which lay you out, I won't feel comfortable leaving you alone."

"If it will make you feel better."

"It will."

Roger made an appointment to see Maya, whose energy balancing treatments, once again, helped to restore his appetite.

Life Way Crisis

I observed the four days of reverence following the ceremony, once again experiencing rushes of memories into my consciousness and spinal releases with emotional catharses, as had happened after the first two ceremonies. Christine comforted me. Having participated in Native American and Aboriginal rituals and processed her own spiritual energetic clearing, she was able to relate to the pain. Her hands-on energy healing helped me through periods of intense release. The dark night of the soul that followed the Life Way would come and go in periodic bursts throughout the next year. I would be reborn from the inside out. At times the emotional and physical pain went so deep that it felt as if the cells in my body were being transformed, as wave after wave of past-life energies came forward to be released, and I cried them out into the universe.

Midway through August Christine returned home, and Roger and I made arrangements to return to Dallas. Additional testing revealed my husband's sensitivities to metals and a low T-cell count. He ordered the appropriate antigens for his metals sensitivities and tested for the autogenous lymphocytic factor (ALF) vaccine, which it was hoped, would address the low T-cell count. Returning to Santa Fe, he added the new antigens and ALF to his treatment program.

20 FULL CIRCLE: HEALING AND CLOSURE

January 2007 through March 2008

In 2007, as a result of the introspective work I had been doing, I came face to face with the emotion that had terrified me most, an emotion I had been denying for years—anger. During some of the dark nights that occurred in this period, it was this emotion that came forward for recognition and release. The unpredictability of the releases frightened me, and the nature of the anger itself was outside of my present experience as a woman. Sometimes, in the visions of this period, I saw myself on ancient battlefields, where men engaged in hand-to-hand combat, fighting for hegemony or defending their lands, their homes, and their women and children against trespass. It was then I thought I knew how an enraged bull feels as it stands pawing the ground, eyeing the red cape of the matador, and then rushing headlong into death. Other times, as the visions unfolded, I felt the deeply rooted anger of women through the ages who had been punished simply for being women—for bearing the fruit of forced sexual liaisons or for merely being suspected of illicit behavior and then living the rest of their lives in disgrace.

School for Experience

It was about this time that one of the local movie channels Roger and I watch was showing *The Magdalene Sisters*. During the scene in the communal shower area, rage overwhelmed me. I guess it was more like outrage than rage. The pain in my heart chakra was intense.

What am I feeling?

Your pain and the pain of others.

Despite the pain, I couldn't stop watching. When the film ended, I ran to my meditation chair, sobbing.

Jesus, are you here?

Always, Jennie.

Thank you, Jesus. Why are we so cruel to each other?

Think of the earth as a school for experience.

Oh, Deborah and Christine have said the same thing to me.

Yes, Spirit speaks to you through the people in your life. As for your question, souls come to earth to experience emotions. They experience these emotions as a result of the events in their lives. Sometimes, the people you consider your greatest persecutors are your greatest teachers.

Deborah did tell me that when I was living in Dallas. I didn't understand it then. I'm not sure I do now.

You do understand. Look inside.

The man who molested me when I was a little girl...he was my teacher?

Yes. It is not the experience. It is what you learn from the experience. Have you forgiven him? Look into your heart.

Yes. I have forgiven him.

Then you have learned an important lesson. Healing comes from forgiveness

LDA Therapy for Roger

Roger continued to struggle with his recovery from exposure to environmental toxins. By April 2007 his gastrointestinal system had nearly returned to normal, but eczema, which had been localized to his back and ankles, began to spread, his fatigue was more pronounced, and brain fog was intermittent. He was unsteady on his feet and needed the aid of a cane to walk. Because the trips to Texas had become too draining for him, when it was time for Roger to retest his ALF serum, we contacted W.A. Shrader, Jr., M.D., a physician whose practice is in Santa Fe. A fellow of the American Academy of Environmental Medicine and a colleague of Dr. Rea, Dr. Shrader agreed to retest the ALF serum in his offices. After meeting with Dr. Shrader, who developed low-dose antigen (LDA) therapy for allergies after it became apparent the FDA would not approve the use of enzyme potentiated desensitization (EPD), used since the 1960s in the United Kingdom, Roger decided to add LDA therapy to his treatment plan. Although his healing path now included a byway on which I had not walked, we walked it together. Between June and November 2007, Roger had three LDA treatments, each of which triggered depression. After the first two treatments, we noticed a worsening of symptoms, followed by a brief remission, after which the symptoms returned. It was the third treatment that seemed to help him turn a corner. The detoxification period afterward was intense, but during the recovery period Roger noticed that his eczema began to clear, his fatigue lessened, and he became steady on his feet once again. He put his cane away. Dr. Shrader, after reviewing Roger's history, decided to suspend treatment until the recurrence of symptoms.

Deborah's Prediction

In March 2008, Roger was well enough for us to have our first "date" since we were poisoned by pesticides in New Orleans in August 2002. We attended a play in the theater of a museum in Santa Fe and then went out for dinner. The enormity of our foray into the normal social world will be readily apparent to anyone struggling with environmental illness. For those outside the EI world, a note of explanation: works of art can outgas certain toxins that may affect people with EI. Carpeting can outgas formaldehyde or toxins from cleaning agents that contain petrochemicals. Patrons can be wearing colognes or aftershave that can bother those with sensitivities to scents. Public buildings are often treated with pesticides and can be poorly ventilated, concentrating exposure. We arrived at the museum early enough so that we could view the art on display and choose end-of-row seats in the theater. Just before the lights dimmed, a woman wearing cologne chose to seat herself in our row. I noted her presence, wondering if Roger would say anything. He did not. I used a visualization I had learned in Dallas to expand my energy fields in an effort to mitigate the strong scent of the cologne. At the moment the scent disappeared from my consciousness, a feeling of sorrow washed over me. Just then I remembered sitting in the auditorium during my son's graduation four years earlier and thinking of what Deborah had said to me early in my healing journey. Those words, of which I was skeptical at first, came back to me clearly.

"One day you'll be in a crowded theater and scented people will be all around you. Instead of being disturbed by the scent of a woman near you, you will feel her sadness."

Well, I thought, *it really has happened.* Surrounding the sadness with light, I sent it out to the universe. Sending love to the woman in our row, I settled down to watch the performance.

EPILOGUE

Throughout 2008 I continued to open to the realm of the soul. I realized that I had long ago joined the ranks of those whom Caroline Myss describes as "monks without monasteries" in *Entering the Castle: An Inner Path to God and Your Soul*. I knew that I was being called to service. I didn't know what form that service would take, but I sensed in my heart that the dark nights through past lives were leading me to a new future. At first I thought that I would guide others to healing and awakening through the books I would write. By the end of 2008, I had already begun thinking about my next book, even as I was approaching agents and publishers about publishing my healing story. Since being certified in *Reiki* level II, however, I had been sending *Reiki* and intuitive energy healing to family and friends. The more I worked in the energetic realm with others, the more I felt called to do more than write about the experience. In early 2009, I asked several people who were struggling with illness to be pro bono clients. As I interacted with these clients, my ability to work in the energetic realm grew, and my clients benefited from the healing relationship. I, however, began to feel very tired. In June, I attended a weekend seminar at the Arasini Foundation's A Healing Place. During one of the breaks between sessions, Deborah asked me how I was feeling. I had long experience with Deborah's questions. They were never accidental.

"I'm really tired."

"Something needs to change, Jennie."

"Deborah, may I call you?"

"Of course."

After I returned home, I placed a call to Deborah. She had already assessed the impact of my work with clients on my body.

"Jennie, you're not clearing yourself adequately. You're taking on too much from the people with whom you've been working."

"That makes sense. When I first started the work, I felt good. Now, I am always exhausted."

"Are you distinguishing between your energies and your clients' and clearing yourself as you work?"

"I'm not. I've just been clearing afterwards."

As we talked, I knew I needed to learn to do the work in a different way. I applied for admittance to the Arasini Foundation's apprenticeship healing program for certification in energy balancing and was accepted. For me, it was a return to my spiritual home; only now, having been on a long journey, I was returning not as a client but as a healer.

I've long since recovered from the symptoms that sent me to Dr. Rea's clinic, as well as from those that plagued me throughout my adult life. Fibromyalgia, with its acute relentless muscle pain, gastro-esophageal reflux disease with its unending burning, lactose intolerance with its discomfort tied to difficulty in digesting dairy products, reactive hypoglycemia with its unstable blood sugar levels sometimes leading to loss of consciousness, recurrent vaginal yeast infections with their burning and pain—all these are now a part of my past. EMF sensitivity, which I first thought of as disability and illness, I now view as my gateway to the energetic realm of the soul. As Deborah predicted would happen one day, I have turned that sensitivity into a tool I use to help other people. I now view health and illness with new eyes, eyes that see beyond the physical world to the wholeness that is ours to claim. The road I chose to walk is far from easy, but it has led me not only to freedom from environmental and other chronic illnesses but also to a path of higher consciousness and to progressive recognition of my soul tasks for this lifetime. Nevertheless, even though I communicate with and perceive the realm of the soul, I am grounded in the secular world and work on my personal soul process, sometimes alone and sometimes through the people I meet. To all those who have walked my path with me, I express my gratitude, whether our interactions can be viewed in the secular world as positive or negative. In truth, because We are One, each interaction provides opportunities for growth. Blessings of light and love to all.

AFTERWORD

Jennie, my wife, asked me to write a postscript to her book in order to provide another physician's perspective on her experience (and later mine) of environmental illness. My training in internal medicine and cardiology led to a career spent mainly in research and teaching, but with enough clinical practice to keep me in touch with general trends in medicine.

I first met Dr. Rea one week after Jennie began treatment under his supervision. I was immediately struck by his understanding of her illness and his confidence that she would recover under his care. I had no previous knowledge or experience of the developing field of environmental medicine, of which Dr. Rea is one of the leading pioneers. His explanation of Jennie's condition was both coherent and convincing. Thereafter, I was present at one in three of Jennie's weekly consultations with him. I gradually became aware of the ever-increasing importance of this hitherto neglected area of medicine. Even at this time (2002/2003), there was little awareness in mainstream medicine of either the problem or the treatment of this debilitating and devastating condition.

Despite following Dr. Rea's instructions to the letter, Jennie's experience was checkered for the first several months, but never once did I have reason to doubt Dr. Rea's understanding and management of her manifold problems. Later, I met the energy healers to whom Dr. Rea had referred Jennie for treatment of the disabling sensitivity to electromagnetic fields that occurs in some patients during detoxification, of which Jennie was unfortunate to be one. I was equally impressed with Deborah Singleton and her healing team's understanding of this issue and their approach to its management.

Only after I retired from my academic position at the end of 2003 and joined Jennie in Santa Fe, did I become fully aware of the G.I. symptoms which Dr. Rea later diagnosed as chemical sensitivity. In fact he said he had been expecting me to develop problems as a result of my living in our condominium for seventeen months after Jennie's acute exposure. After testing for a wide range of potential sensitivities and taking appropriate vaccines, my symptoms began to abate, but I was unable to regain the weight I had lost as a result of an attack of shingles in 2003. Because I found myself increasingly tired and no longer able to make regular visits to Texas, I then came under the care of a colleague of Dr. Rea, Dr. Shrader, in Santa Fe. I also followed Jennie's suggestion that I receive energy balancing from Maya Page. My appetite gradually improved, and I regained most of the weight I had lost.

In summary, I would like to express my appreciation of the specialists in the emerging field of Environmental Medicine, which has had such profoundly beneficial effects, first for my wife and then for me.

Roger Sherwin

BOOKS MENTIONED IN THE TEXT

Baker-Laporte, Paula, AIA; Erica Elliott, M.D.; and John Banta, B.A. *Prescriptions for A Healthy House: A Practical Guide for Architects, Builders & Homeowners.* British Columbia, Canada: New Society Publishers, 2001.

Bernstein, Jerome. *Living in the Borderland: The Evolution of Consciousness and the Challenge of Healing Trauma.* London and New York: Routledge, Taylor and Francis Group, 2005.

Bower, John. *The Healthy House: How to Buy One, How to Build One, How to Cure a Sick One.* Fourth Edition. Bloomington, Indiana: The Healthy House Institute, 2001.

Brennan, Barbara Ann. *Hands of Light: A Guide to Healing through the Human Energy Field.* New York: Bantam Books, June 1988.

—. *Light Emerging: The Journey of Personal Healing.* New York: Bantam Books, December 1993.

Eden, Donna, with David Feinstein. *Energy Medicine.* New York: Jeremy P. Tarcher/Putnam, 1998.

Gold, Peter. *Navajo & Tibetan Sacred Wisdom: The Circle of the Spirit.* Rochester, Vermont: Inner Traditions International, 1994.

Gorman, Carolyn, with Marie Hyde. *Less Toxic Alternatives.* Texarkana, Texas: Optimum Publishing, 2001.

McVicker, Marilyn. *Sauna Detoxification Therapy: A Guide for the Chemically Sensitive.* Jefferson, North Carolina: McFarland & Company, Inc., Publishers, 1997.

Myss, Caroline, Ph.D. *Entering the Castle: An Inner Path to God and Your Soul.* New York: Free Press, 2007.

Pert, Candace B., Ph.D. *Molecules of Emotion.* New York: Scribner, Simon & Schuster, 1997.

Rea, William J., M.D., F.A.C.S., F.A.A.E.M. *Chemical Sensitivity, vols. 1-4.* London and New York: CRC-Press, Taylor & Francis, 1992-1996.

Rogers, Sherry A., M.D *Detoxify or Die.* Sarasota, Florida: Sand

Key Company, 2002.

—. *The E.I. Syndrome Revised: An Rx for Environmental Illness.* Sarasota, Florida: Sand Key Company, 1995.

Tolle, Eckhart. *A New Earth: Awakening to Your Life's Purpose.* New York: Plume, Penguin Group, 2006.

—. *The Power of Now: A Guide to Spiritual Enlightenment.* Canada: Namaste Publishing, 1997, and Novato, California: New World Library, 1999.

SUGGESTIONS FOR FURTHER READING

Batie, Howard F., Mh.D. *Healing Body, Mind, & Spirit: A Guide to Energy-Based Healing*. Woodbury, Minnesota: Llewellyn Publications, 2003.

Bruce, Robert. *Energy Work: The Secret of Healing and Spiritual Development*. Charlottesville, Virginia: Hampton Roads Publishing Company, Inc., 2007.

Gilkeson, Jim. *Energy Healing: A Pathway to Inner Growth*. New York: Marlowe & Company, 2000.

Grof, Stanislav, M.D. *The Transpersonal Vision: The Healing Potential of Nonordinary States of Consciousness*. Bolder, Colorado: Sounds True, 1998.

Hay, Louise L. *You Can Heal Your Life*. Carlsbad, California: Hay House, Inc., 1984.

Hawkes, Joyce Whiteley, Ph.D. *Cell-Level Healing: The Bridge from Soul to Cell*. New York: Atria Books, 2006.

James, John, Ph.D. *The Great Field: Soul at Play in a Conscious Universe*. Fulton, California: Elite Books, 2007.

Judith, Anodea. *Eastern Body Western Mind: Psychology and the Chakra System as a Path to the Self*. Berkeley, California: Celestial Arts, 1996, 2004 (revised).

McTaggart, Lynne. *The Intention Experiment*. New York: Free Press, 2007.

Mehl-Madrona, Lewis, M.D. *Coyote Medicine*. New York: Scribner, Simon & Schuster, Inc., 1997.

—. *Narrative Medicine: The Use of History and Story in the Healing Process*. Rochester, Vermont: Bear & Company, 2007

Millar, Myrna, B. Ed., M.B.A., and Heather Millar, B.S.N., R.N. *The Toxic Labyrinth*. Vancouver, Canada: NICO Professional Services, 1995.

Murphy, Marcia. *Healing Environmental Illness from Within*. British Columbia, Canada: Trafford Publishing, 2003.

Myss, Caroline, Ph.D. *Invisible Acts of Power: Channeling Grace in Your Everyday Life*. New York: Free Press, 2004.

—. *Sacred Contracts: Awakening Your Divine Potential*. New York: Three Rivers Press, 2003.

—. *Why People Don't Heal and How They Can*. New York: Three Rivers Press, 1997.

Ober, Clinton, Stephen T. Sinatra, and Martin Zucker. *Earthing: The Most Important Health Discovery Ever?* Laguna Beach, California: Basic Health Publications, 2010.

Pogačnik, Marko. *Healing the Heart of the Earth*. Scotland, UK: Findhorn Press, 1997.

Rea, William, J., M.D., FACS, FAAEM. *Optimum Environments for Optimum Health & Creativity: Designing and Building a Healthy Home or Office*. Dallas, Texas: Crown Press, Inc., 2002.

Sampson, Robert, M.D., and Patricia Hughes, B.S.N. *Breaking Out of Environmental Illness*. Santa Fe, New Mexico: Bear and Company Publishing, 1997.

Smith, Lorraine. *Heal Environmental Illness and Reclaim Your Life*. Chelmsford, Massachusetts: Diveena Publications, 2000.

Temple-Thurston, Leslie, with Brad Laughlin. *The Marriage of Spirit: Enlightened Living in Today's World*. Santa Fe, New Mexico: CoreLight Publications, 2000.

— *Returning to Oneness: The Seven Keys of Ascension*. Santa Fe, New Mexico: CoreLight Publishing, 2002.

Topf, Linda Noble, with Hal Zina Bennett, Ph.D. *You Are Not Your Illness*. New York: Simon & Schuster, 1995.

HELPFUL RESOURCES

A Healing Place (1-972-437-5332) — www.ahealingplace.org: education and wellness center founded and directed by Deborah Singleton offering energy balancing sessions, personal and spiritual counseling, education outreach, individualized guidance in meditation, yoga, and body work therapy, as well as an apprenticeship program

American Academy of Environmental Medicine — www. aaemonline.org: provides research and education in the recognition, treatment, and prevention of illnesses induced by exposures to biological and chemical agents in air, food, and water; website features directory by state of doctors of environmental medicine, links to other organizations, and access to physician and patient education

American Environmental Health Foundation (1-800-428-2343) — www.aehf.com: air purifiers and filters, bedding, books, clothing, home improvement, household cleaning, lawn and garden, medical supplies, nutritional supplements, personal care products, pollution detection kits, water filtration

Bright Future Futon Company (1-505-268-9738) — www.bluelotusyoga.com: beds, bedding, mattresses, yoga mats; ordering a futon or mattress without flame retardant requires a prescription

Casa Natura (1-505-820-7634) — www.casanaturaorganic.com: furniture and home accents, beds, mattresses, bedding, towels, bath mats, bath robes, clothing

Chemical Injury Information Network — www.ciin.org: support and advocacy organization for those with MCS, links to environmental lawyers, groups, information, home of Our Toxic Times

Cole, Carol, Ph.D., LMFT (1-972-437-5870) — www.drcarolcole .com: psycho-spiritual counselor

Eco House Santa Fe (1-505-699-7080)—www.ecohousesantafe .com: design and construction of environmentally friendly houses, using natural materials and innovative design to maintain pristine indoor air quality

Environmental Health Center-Dallas (1-214-368-4132)— www.ehcd.com: center founded and directed by Dr. William J. Rea providing testing for chemical sensitivity and allergies, diagnosis of environmental and other chronic illnesses as well as sensitivity to electro-magnetic fields, antigen preparation, sauna detoxification, massage and physical therapy, immunotherapy, nutritional counseling, psychological counseling

Environmental Health Network—www.ehnca.org: advocacy organization with extensive links to resources and information on EI, EMF, MCS, and chronic illnesses; follow EHN on Facebook

Environmental Illness Resources—www.ei-resource.org: U.K.-based website for environmental illness and multiple chemical sensitivity

Elliott, Erica, M.D. (1-505-471-8531)—www.ericaelliottmd.com: Santa Fe-based family practice and environmental medicine, office and telephone consultations by appointment

Gaiam—www.gaiam.com: clothing, furniture, household cleaning, and personal products

Green Homes for Sale—www.GreenHomesForSale.com: eco, green, healthy homes for sale; listings detail materials used in construction; includes a by-state finder

Heart Gifts (1-972-989-2591)—www.aheartgift.com: heart rocks, crystal gemstones, and heart-shaped stones made of natural minerals, used to share love, healing, and joy

Human Ecology Action League—www.healnatl.org.: source for information on environment and health, home of the Human Ecologist, resource for creating healthy less-toxic environments, articles on allergies, asthma, MCS, fibromyalgia, chronic fatigue syndrome, food intolerances

Janice's—www.janices.com: bedding, clothing, personal care products, air and water purifiers

MCSurvivors—www.MCSurvivors.com: online forum for MCS/EI survivors to exchange stories and provide support for each other

National Allergy Products—www.natlallergy.com: air filtration, allergen control, bedding, personal care products, safer cleaning products

Nutriwellness (1-972-239-1148)—www.nutriwellness.com: Chris and Dr. Ron Overberg, nutritional counseling via office and phone consultations, affordable testing and nutritional treatment for patients with environmental, gluten, and celiac challenges

Organic Mall—www.organicmall.com: directory of websites of retail and wholesale sellers of clothing and personal care products for people as well as products for pets

Organic Skin Care (1-505-474-4310)—www.organicskincare-santafe.com: holistic spa treatments using natural and organic (naturally scented) products; retails a variety of natural and organic skin care products

Planet Thrive—www.planetthrive.com: articles, resources, and an online community for people recovering from chemical sensitivity, lyme disease, mold illness, chronic fatigue syndrome, fibromyalgia, electrical sensitivity, and other environmentally based illnesses

Reshelter—www.reshelter.org: 501 (c) (3) non-profit charity formed to address the housing crisis for those displaced by environmental intolerances

Reshelter Housing Ads—www.reshelter.org/housing-ads: free safer housing listings

Rogers, Sherry, M.D.—www.prestigepublishing.com: site for ordering books written by Dr. Rogers, for accessing her newsletters, and for making appointments for non-patient telephone consultations

Sachi Organics—www.sachiorganics.com: platform beds, futons, mattresses, yoga props, linens, bed pillows, furniture, nursery; ordering a futon or mattress without flame retardant requires a prescription; e-mail questions to service@sachior-ganics.com

Santa Fe Center for Allergy and Environmental Medicine (1-505-983-8890)—www.drshrader.com: center founded and directed by Dr. W. Shrader: allergy and environmental medicine, low dose antigen (LDA) therapy

Contact Jennie Sherwin through info@jenniesherwin.com. Visit Jennie's book and energy practice website at www.jenniesh-erwin.com.